MW01099002

تعلم العربية

TEACH YOURSELF ARABIC

Published by
Sterling Publishers Private Limited

LANGUAGE IN USE

تعلّم العربية

TEACH YOURSELF ARABIC

Dr Z. A. Farooqi
Dr Habibullah Khan

A Sterling Paperback

STERLING PAPERBACKS
An imprint of
Sterling Publishers (P) Ltd.
L-10, Green Park Extension, New Delhi-110016
Tel : 6191023, 6191784/85; Fax : 91-11-6190028
E-mail: ghai@nde.vsnl.net.in
Website : www.sterlingpublishers.com

Teach Yourself Arabic

ISBN 81 207 2084 9
Reprint 2000

Published by Sterling Publishers Pvt. Ltd., New Delhi-110016.
Laserset at Pharos Media & Publishing (P) Ltd., New Delhi-110025
Printed at Ram Printograph (India), Delhi-110051

PREFACE

Globalization has rendered the world a small village and greatly enhanced the need for closer communication. This endeavour represents a modest response to that need. A new approach to the teaching and learning of a foreign language in a short duration for better understanding has never been as intensely needed as it is now. Attempts have, therefore, been made over a few decades to innovate ways and means to teach a foreign language exclusively keeping in view the time factor. This book is a step forward in that direction.

Broadly divided into three parts, it has specifically been designed for tourists, businessmen and students who have never had an opportunity to study Arabic or those who have studied it at school level and would like to improve their language skill. The first part deals with the minimum and the simplest rules of grammar that are indispensable in the learning of Arabic while complicated rules have deliberately been avoided. Grammatical rules are followed by examples and necessary exercises. The second part is divided into a number of units. Each unit deals with a particular theme such as introduction, marketing, travelling and similar live situations, which the tourists, businessmen and students are likely to come across during their stay in Arabic-speaking countries. It also contains an additional list of words relating to select topics with a view to enhancing the vocabulary of the reader. Since the book is aimed at imparting basic communicative skills in spoken language, preference, at many places, has been given to the colloquial form of words and expressions generally used by the Arabs and their pronunciations are given as they are spoken. For example the word هندى *has been given as* Hindi *instead of* Hindiun. *However, for the benefit of the learners who are not acquainted with the 'International Phonetic Alphabet' the easiest method of pronunciation has been adopted.*

In the end we wish to express our sincere thanks to Mr S.K. Ghai, Mg. Director, Sterling Publishers Pvt. Ltd., who has been instrumental behind this project. Thanks are also due to Dr Zafarul-Islam Khan and his staff for excellent typesetting of the book. Finally we request the readers to give us feedback as it will help us improve the book in its next edition.

AUTHORS

CONTENTS

THE ARABIC ALPHABET

Arabic is one of the Semitic group of languages. It is written from right to left. The alphabet consists of 29 letters (if *hamza* is counted as a separate letter). It has no concept of capital or small letters. But the letters assume variant forms according to their postitions: isolated, initial, medial or final. These are explained clearly in the following tables.

THE ALPHABET

ا	Alif	a	ض	Ḍād	ḍ
ء	Hamza	و	ط	Ṭā	ṭ
ب	Bā	b	ظ	Ẓā	ẓ
ت	Tā	t	ع	Ain	ᶜ
ث	Thā	th	غ	Ghain	gh
ج	Jeem	j	ف	Fā	f
ح	Ḥā	ḥ	ق	Qāf	q
خ	Khā	kh	ك	Kāf	k
د	Dāl	d	ل	Lām	l
ذ	Dhāl	dh	م	Meem	m
ر	Rā	r	ن	Noon	n
ز	Zā	z	ه	Hā	h
س	Seen	s	و	Waw	w
ش	Sheen	sh	ي	Yā	y
ص	Ṣād	ṣ			

1 - The letter ث is pronounced in Arabic like th in the English words: thank, think.

2 - The letter ذ (dh) is pronounced in Arabic like th in the Eghlish words: this, these.

3 - The letter ص (ṣ) is pronounced by the tongue being set against the palate instead of the teeth.

4 - The letter ض (ḍ) is an emphatic d sound produced by the tongue being set against the palate instead of the teeth.

5 - The letter ط (ṭ) is an emphatic t sound produced as mentioned above.

6 - The letter ظ (ẓ) is also an emphatic z sound produced as mentioned above.

7 - The letter ع (ʿ) is a very strong guttural sound produced by the compression of the throat and the expulsion of the breath.

8 - The letter غ (gh) has a sound like the gargling pronunciation between g and r.

9 - The letter ق (q) is a k sound produced in the throat.

The variant forms of the letters according to their positions: isolated, initial, medial, and final

Isolated	Initial	Medial	Final	Examples
ا	ا	ـا	ـا	ابا
ب	بـ	ـبـ	ـب	ببب
ت	تـ	ـثـ	ـث	ثثث
ج	جـ	ـجـ	ـج	ججج
ح	حـ	ـحـ	ـح	ححح
خ	خـ	ـخـ	ـخ	خخخ
د	د	ـد	ـد	ددد/شديد
ذ	ذ	ـذ	ـذ	ذذذ/لذيذ
ر	ر	ـر	ـر	ررر/بريد
ز	ز	ـز	ـز	ززز/غزل
س	سـ	ـسـ	ـس	سسس
ش	شـ	ـشـ	ـش	ششش
ص	صـ	ـصـ	ـص	صصص
ض	ضـ	ـضـ	ـض	ضضض
ط	ضـ	ـطـ	ـط	ططط
ظ	ظـ	ـظـ	ـظ	ظظظ
ع	عـ	ـعـ	ـع	ععع
غ	غـ	ـغـ	ـغ	غغغ
ف	فـ	ـفـ	ـف	ففف
ق	قـ	ـقـ	ـق	ققق
ك	كـ	ـكـ	ـك	ككك
ل	لـ	ـلـ	ـل	للل
م	مـ	ـمـ	ـم	ممم
ن	نـ	ـنـ	ـن	ننن
ه	هـ	ـهـ	ـه	ههه
و	و	ـو	ـو	ووو/وهو
ي	يـ	ـيـ	ـي	ييي

THE VOWELS

S.N.	Name of the vowel	Sign of the vowel	English equivalent	Examples
1	Fatha (Short vowel)	بَ bā	a	بَبَبَ (ba ba ba) لَكَ (laka)
2	Ḍamma (S.v)	بُ bū	u	بُبُبُ (bu bu bu)
3	Kasra (S.v)	بِ bī	i	بِبِبِ (bi bi bi)
4	Alif (Long vowel)	با baa	aa	بَابَ (baaba)
5	Waw (L.v)	بُو boo	oo	بُوبَ (booba)
6	Yaa (L.v)	بِى bee	ee	بِيبَ (beeba)
7	Sukoon	بْ	absence of any vowel	بُبْ (bub) بَبْ (bab) بِبْ (bib)
8	Madda	آ		آبَ (aaba) آمَنَ (aamana)
9	Shadda	بّ	Sign of double consonant	بَبَّ (babba) رَبَّ (rabba)
10	Tanween	بً ban بٌ bun بٍ bin	an un in	بَابًا (baban) بَابٌ (babun) بَابٍ (babin)

(1) Whenever a consonant is without vowel, it receives the sign (ْ) above it. For example قُلْتُ (*Qultu*). It indicates the absence of any vowel.

EXERCISE IN READING

بَ (ba)	بِ (bi)	بُ (bu)	بَبِبُ (babibu)	بَبِبٌ (babibun)
تَ (ta)	تِ (ti)	تُ (tu)	تِتَتُ (titatu)	تِتَتٌ (titatun)
ثَ (tha)	ثِ (thi)	ثُ (thu)	ثَثِثُ (tha thi thu)	ثَثِثٌ (tha thi thun)
جَ (ja)	جِ (ji)	جُ (ju)	جَجِجُ (jajiju)	
حَ (ḥa)	حِ (ḥi)	حُ (ḥu)		
خَ (kha)	خِ (khi)	خُ (khu)		
دَ (da)	دِ (di)	دُ (du)	دَدِدٌ (da di dun)	
ذَ (dha)	ذِ (dhi)	ذُ (dhu)		
رَ (ra)	رِ (ri)	رُ (ru)	رَرِرٌ (ra ri run)	
زَ (za)	زِ (zi)	زُ (zu)		
سَ (sa)	سِ (si)	سُ (su)	سَسِسٌ (sa si sun)	
شَ (sha)	شِ (shi)	شُ (shu)	شَشِشٌ (sha shi shun)	
صَ (ṣa)	صِ (ṣi)	صُ (ṣu)		
ضَ (ḍa)	ضِ (ḍi)	ضُ (ḍhu)	ضَضِضٌ (ḍaḍiḍun)	
طَ (ṭa)	طِ (ṭi)	طُ (ṭu)		
ظَ (ẓa)	ظِ (ẓi)	ظُ (ẓu)	ظَظِظٌ (ẓaẓiẓun)	
عَ (ʿa)	عِ (ʿi)	عُ (ʿu)	عَعِعٌ (ʿa ʿi ʿun)	
غَ (gha)	غِ (ghi)	غُ (ghu)	غَغِغٌ (gha ghi ghun)	
فَ (fa)	فِ (fi)	فُ (fu)	فَفِفٌ (fa fi fun)	
قَ (qa)	قِ (qi)	قُ (qu)	قَقِقٌ (qa qi qun)	
كَ (ka)	كِ (ki)	كُ (ku)	كَكِكٌ (ka ki kun)	
لَ (la)	لِ (li)	لُ (lu)	لَلِلٌ (la li lun)	
مَ (ma)	مِ (mi)	مُ (mu)	مَمِمٌ (ma mi mun)	
نَ (na)	نِ (na)	نُ (nu)	نَنِنٌ (na ni nun)	
هَ (ha)	هِ (hi)	هُ (hu)	هَهِهٌ (ha hi hun)	

EXERCISE IN READING

بَلْ (bal)	قُلْ (qul)	طِبْ (ṭib)
سِرْ (sir)	لا (laa)	مَا (maa)
لَمْ (lam)	عَنْ (ʿan)	ذُو (ḍhoo)
يَدٌ (yadun)	كُلُّ (kullu)	دَلَّ (dalla)
طِبٌّ (ṭibbun)	لُبٌّ (lubbun)	بَيْتاً (baitan)
بَيْتٍ (baitin)	فِى (fi)	عَلَى (ʿala)
حَسَنٌ (hasanun)	فِيْلٌ (feelun)	كَتَبَتْ (katabat)
كَاتِبٌ (katibun)	اتَّخَذْتَ (ittakhaḍta)	تَتَذَكَّرُ (tatadhakkaru)
ثَبَتَ (thabata)	جَحِيْمٌ (jaheemun)	دَخَلَ (dakhala)
رَحْمٰنُ (raḥmanu)	قُطُبٌ (quṭubun)	كَلاَمٌ (lalamun)
قَلَمٌ (qalamun)	لَهُ (lahu)	مَعَهَا (maʿaha)

THE GENDER

All the nouns in Arabic are either masculine or feminine. Normally the male is masculine and the female is feminine as أبٌ (abun) father and أُمٌّ (ummun) mother.

But the gender in Arabic grammar is not necessarily connected with male or female. Lifeless objects too are treated as masculine or feminine. The following guide lines can help determine the gender of any object.

1 - Inanimate objects ending with ة are feminine.

Example: نـافِذَةٌ (naafidhatun) "a window" مِرْوَحَـةٌ (mirwaḥatun) "a fan".

2 - Normally a feminine word is formed by adding ة at the end of masculine. Example:

Masculine	*Feminine*
طَالِبٌ (ṭalibun) a student	طَالِبَةٌ (ṭalibatun) a female student
مُعَلِّمٌ (muᶜallimun) a teacher	مُعَـلِّمَةٌ (muᶜallimatun) a female teacher

3 - Names of lands and cites like Egypt, Kuwait, Beirut are normally feminine.

4 - Parts of the body which are in pairs are feminine. Example: يَدٌ (yadun) 'hand' رِجْلٌ (rijlun) 'leg'.

5 - The following nouns are treated as feminine:

أَرْضٌ (arḍun) 'earth' بِئْرٌ (bi-run) 'well' حَرْبٌ (ḥarbun) 'war' خَمْرٌ (khamrun) 'wine' دَارٌ (darun) 'house' رِيحٌ (reeḥun) 'wind' شَمْسٌ (shamsun) 'sun'.

PERSONAL PRONOUNS (1)

English	Arabic	Pronunciation
I (msc/fem/sng)	أَنَا	anaa
We(msc/fem/ dual/plural)	نَحْنُ	naḥnu
You (msc/sng)	أَنْتَ	anta
You all(msc/plu)	أَنْتُمْ	antum
You (fem/sng)	أَنْتِ	anti
You all (fem/plu)	أَنْتُنَّ	antunna
He	هُوَ	huwa
They (msc)	هُمْ	hum
She	هِيَ	hiya
They (fem)	هُنَّ	hunna

(1) Dual form is avoided at this stage

EXERCISE

I am an Indian.	أَنَا هِندِى	anaa hindee
We are tourists.	نَحْنُ سُوَّاحْ	naḥnu suwwah
You are a doctor.	أَنْتَ طَبِيْب	anta ṭabeeb
You all are businessmen.	أَنْتُمْ تُجَّار	antum tujjar
You (fem) are a doctor.	أَنْتِ طَبِيبة	anti tabeeba
He is an engineer.	هُوَ مُهَنْدِس	huwa muhandis
She is a nurse.	هِيَ مُمَرِّضَة	hiya mumarrida

VOCABULARY

1 - Indian هِندِى hindee

2 - Tourist سائح Sayeh (pl. Suyyah / suwwah)

3 - Doctor طَبِيْب ṭabeeb

4 - Businessman تَاجِرْ tajir (pl. tujjar)

5 - Engineer مُهَنْدس muhandis

6 - Nurse مُمَرِّضة mumarrida (pl. mumarriḍat)

DEMONSTRATIVE PRONOUNS [1]

English	Arabic	Pronunciation
This (masc)	هذا	haadaa
This (fem)	هذِهِ	haadhihee
These (masc & fem)	هؤُلاَء	haawulaaye
That (masc)	ذلِكَ	dhaalika
That (fem)	تِلْكَ	tilka
Those	أُولئِكَ	uoolayika

(1) Dual form is avoided at this stage.

EXERCISE

This is an airport.	هذا مَطَار	haaḍa mataar
This is a car.	هذه سَيَارَة	hadhihee sayyara
These people are businessmen.	هؤلاَءْ الرِجَالُ تُجَّار	haawulaaye rrijaal tujjar
That is a hotel.	ذلِكَ فُنْدُق	dhaalika funduq
That is a truck.	تلكَ شاحِنة	tilka shahina
Those people are tourists.	أُولئِك الناس سُيّاح	uoolayika nnaas suyyah

VOCABULARY

7 - Airport	مَطَار	maṭaar
8 - Car	سَيّارة	sayyara / pl.: sayyarat
9 - Pen	قلمْ	qalam / pl.: aqlaam
10 - Note Book	دَفترْ	daftar / pl.: dafaatir
11 - Bag	حَقِيْبَة	haqeeba / pl.: haqayib
12 - Hotel	فندُق	funduq / pl.: fanaadiq
13 - Truck	شَاحِنة	shaahina / pl.: shaahinat
14 - Office	مكتَبْ	maktab / pl.: makaatib
15 - Chair	كرْسِى	kursee / pl.: karaasee
16 - Suitcase	شَنطة	shanta

INTERROGATIVE PARTICLES

English	Arabic	Pronunciation
What	مَا / هَل / أ	maa / hal / a
Who	مَنْ	man
Where	أيْنَ	aina
How	كَيْفَ	kaifa
When	مَتى	mataa
Whom / Whose	لِمَنْ	liman
Why	لِماذا	limadhaa
Which	أيٌ / أية	aiyu / aiyatu
How much / How many	كَمْ	kam

EXERCISE

What is this ?	مَا هذا ؟	maa haaḍhaa
Who is this ?	مَنْ هذا ؟	man haaḍhaa
Where is the hotel ?	أيْنَ الفُنْدُق ؟	aina-l-funduq
How is Raj ?	كَيْفَ راج ؟	kaifa Raaj
When is the train ?	مَتى القِطَارُ ؟	mata-l-qitaru
Whose pen is this ?	لِمَنْ هذا القَلَمُ ؟	liman haaḍha-l-qalamu
Why are you here ?	لِماذا أنتَ هنا ؟	limaaḍhaa anta hunaa
Which car ?	أيَّةُ سَيّارة ؟	aiyatu sayyara
How many bags ?	كَمْ حَقِيْبَة ؟	kam haqeeba

VOCABULARY

17 - Train قِطَار qiṭaar

18 - Here هنا hunaa

PRONOMINAL SUFFIXES [1]

English	Arabic	Pronunciation	Examples
my (msc/fem)	ي	ee	my book كِتَابِي kitabee
Our (msc/fem)	نَا	naa	our book كِتَابُنَا kitaabunaa
Your (msc)	كَ	ka	your book كِتَابُكَ kitaabuka
Your (fem)	كِ	ki	Your book كِتَابُكِ kitaabuki
Your (pl./msc)	كُمْ	kum	You people's book كِتَابُكُم kitaabukum
Your (pl.fem)	كُنَّ	kunna	You ladies' book كِتَابُكُنَّ kitaabukunna
His	هُ	hu	His book كِتَابُه kitaabuhu
Their (msc)	هُمْ	hum	Their book كِتَابُهُم kitaabuhum
Her	هَا	haa	Her book كِتَابُها kitaabuhaa
Their	هُنَّ	hunna	Their book كِتَابُهُنَّ kitaabuhunnaa

(1) Dual form is avoided at this stage.

EXERCISE

Where is my book ? أينَ كِتابِي ؟ aina kitaabee

Your book is on the table. كِتابُكَ عَلَى المَكْتَب.
kitaabuka ala-l-maktab

Is it our hotel ? هَلْ هذا فُندُقنا ؟ hal haadhaa funduqunaa

Yes, it is yours. نعَمْ هذا فُندُقُكم . naʿam haaḍhaa funduqukum

Where is your house ? أينَ بَيْتك ؟ aina baituka

My house is in Delhi. بيتِي فِي دلهي . baitee fee delhee

Where is his office ? أينَ مَكْتَبُه ؟ aina maktabuhu

His office is behind the post office مَكْتَبه خلفَ مَكتبِ البَرِيد
maktabuhu khalfa maktabil-bareed

Is it their company? هَلْ هذه شَرِكتُهُمْ؟ hal haaḍhihee sharekatuhum

No, it is not their company. لا، هذه ليستْ شَرِكتَهُمْ .
laa, haḍhihee laisat sharekatahum

Whose factory is it ? لِمَنْ هذا المَصنَعُ؟ liman haaḍhaa-l-masnaʿ

It is her factory. هذا مَصْنَعُها . haaḍhaa masnaʿuhaa

VOCABULARY

19 - Book كِتَاب kitaab

20 - House بَيْت bait

21 - Yes نَعَم naʿam

22 - No لا laa

23 - Office مَكْتَب maktab

24 - Behind خَلْفَ khalfa

25 - Company شَرِكَة shareka

26 - Factory مَصْنَعْ masnaʿ

IMPORTANT PREPOSITIONS / ADVERBIAL ACCUSATIVES, ETC.

English	Arabic	Pronun-ciation	Examples
From	مِنْ	min	From London/min landan
To	إِلى	ila	To Delhi / ila delhee
By	بِ	be	By bus / bel-baas
With	بِ	be	With the pen / bel-qalam
With	مَعَ	ma^c	With you / ma^{c}aka
For	لِ	le	For me / lee
In	فِي	fee	In the room / fil-ghurfa
And	و	Wa	Pen and book / qalam wa kitab
Very	جدّاً	jiddan	This is very tall / haḍhaa taweel jiddan
Now	الآنَ	al-aan	He is absent now/ huwa ghaib al-aan
Also	أيضًا	aiḍan	He also / huwa aiḍan
Because	لأنَّ	leanna	Because you / leannaka
On	عَلى	^{c}ala	On the table/^{c}ala-l-maktab
Above	فَوْقَ	fauqa	Above the table / fauqa-l-maktab
Under	تَحْتَ	taḥta	Under the table/ taḥta-l-maktab
Infront of	أمَامَ	amaama	Infront of the office / amaama-l-maktab
Behind	خَلْفَ	khalfa	Behind the office / khalfa-l-maktab
Before	قَبْلَ	qabla	Before the office / qabla-l-maktab
After	بَعْدَ	ba^{c}da	After the office/ ba^{c}da-l-maktab
Around	حَوْلَ	ḥaula	Around the office / ḥaula-l-maktab
Between	بَيْنَ	baina	Between this and that / baina haaḍhaa wa ḍhaalika
Towards	نَحْوَ	naḥwa	Towards the office / naḥwa-l-maktab

THE USE OF 'HAVE' AND 'HAVE NOT' (1)

English	Arabic	Pronun-ciation	Examples
POSITIVE			
I have	عِندِى	ʿindee	I have a car / ʿindee sayyara
We have	عِندَنا	ʿindanaa	We have a car / ʿindanaa sayyara
You have (msc)	عِندَكَ	ʿindaka	"
You all have	عِندَكُم	ʿindakum	"
You have (fem)	عِندَكِ	ʿindaki	"
You all have (fem)	عِندكُنَّ	ʿindakunna	"
He has	عِندَه	ʿindahoo	"
They have	عِندَهُمْ	ʿindahum	"
She has	عِندَها	ʿindahaa	"
They have	عِندَهُنَّ	ʿindahunna	"

(1) Such expressions can be formulated in many ways such as لى (lee), لَدَيَّ (ladayya), etc.

NEGATIVE [(1)]			
I do not have	لَيْسَ عِنْدِي	laisa ʿindee	I do not have a pen / laisa ʿindee qalam
We do not have	لَيْسَ عِنْدَنا	laisa ʿindanaa	”
You do not have (msc)	لَيْسَ عِنْدَكَ	laisa ʿindaka	”
You do not have (fem)	لَيْسَ عِنْدَكِ	laisa ʿindaki	”
He does not have	لَيْسَ عِنده	laisa ʿindahoo	”
She does not have	لَيْسَ عِنْدها	laisa ʿindaha	”

(1) Such expressions can be formulated in many ways such as ليس لِي (Laisa lee), ليس لدَىّ (Laisa ladayya), etc.

THE USE OF 'CAN' AND 'CANNOT'

English	Arabic	Pronunciation
	CAN	
I can	أنا أَقْدَرْ	anaa aqdar
We can	نَحْنُ نَقْدَرْ	naḥnu naqdar
You can	أَنْتَ تَقْدَرْ	anta taqdar
He can	هُوَ يَقْدَرْ	huwa yaqdar
She can	هِيَ تَقْدَرْ	heya taqdar
They can	هُمْ يَقْدَرُوْن	hum yaqdaroon
	CANNOT	
I cannot	أنا لا أَقْدَرْ	anaa laa aqdar
We cannot	نَحْنُ لا نَقْدَرْ	naḥnu laa naqdar
You cannot	أَنْتَ لا تَقْدَرْ	anta laa taqdar
He cannot	هُوَ لا يَقْدَرْ	huwa laa yaqdar
She cannot	هِيَ لا تَقْدَرْ	heya laa taqdar
They cannot	هُمْ لا يَقْدَرُوْن	hum laa yaqdaroon
	INTERROGATIVE	
Can I...	هَلْ أَقْدَرْ / هل يُمْكِنني	hal aqdar / hal yumkenunee
Can you...	هَلْ تَقْدَرْ / هل يُمْكِنكَ	hal taqdar / hal yumkenuka
Can he...	هَلْ يَقْدَرْ / هل يُمْكِنه	hal yaqdar / hal yumkenuhu etc.

THE CARDINAL NUMBERS

English	Arabic ciphers	Arabic	Pronunciation
0	٠	صِفْرْ	ṣifr
1	١	وَاحِدْ	waaḥid
2	٢	إِثْنَيْنِ	iṭhnain
3	٣	ثَلاثَة	thalaathata
4	٤	أَرْبَعَة	arbaʿa
5	٥	خَمْسَة	khamsa
6	٦	سِتَّة	sittaa
7	٧	سَبْعَة	sabaʿa
8	٨	ثَمانِيَة	thamaaniya
9	٩	تِسْعَة	tisʿa
10	١٠	عَشَرَة	ashara
11	١١	أَحَدَ عَشَرَ	aḥada ashara
12	١٢	إِثْنَا عَشَرَ	ithnaa ashara
13	١٣	ثَلاثَة عَشَرَ	thalaathata ashara
14	١٤	أَرْبَعَة عَشَر	arbaʿata ʿashara
15	١٥	خَمسة عَشَرَ	khamsata ʿashara
16	١٦	سِتَّةَ عَشَرَ	sittata ʿashara
17	١٧	سَبْعَةَ عَشَرَ	sabʿata ʿashara
18	١٨	ثَمانِيَةَ عَشَرَ	thamaniyata ʿashara
19	١٩	تِسْعَةَ عَشَرَ	tisʿata ʿashara

20	٢٠	عِشْرِينَ	iṣhreen
21	٢١	وَاحِدْ وَعِشْرِيْنَ	waḥid wa ishreen
30	٣٠	ثَلاثِيْنَ	thalaatheen
40	٤٠	أَرْبَعِيْنَ	arbaᶜeen
50	٥٠	خَمْسِيْنَ	khamseen
60	٦٠	سِتِّيْنَ	sitteen
70	٧٠	سَبْعِيْنَ	sabᶜeen
80	٨٠	ثَمَانِيْنَ	thamaneen
90	٩٠	تِسْعِيْنَ	tisᶜeen
100	١٠٠	مِائَة	mi'a
200	٢٠٠	مِائَتَيْنِ	mi'atain
300	٣٠٠	ثَلاَثُ مِائَة	thalathu mi'a
400	٤٠٠	أَرْبَعُ مِائَة	arbaᶜu mi'a
500	٥٠٠	خَمْسُ مِائَة	khamsu mi'a
600	٦٠٠	سِتُّ مِائَة	sittu mi'a
700	٧٠٠	سَبْعُ مِائَة	sabᶜu mi'a
800	٨٠٠	ثَمَانِى مِائَة	thamani mi'a
900	٩٠٠	تِسْعُ مِائَة	tisᶜu mi'a
1000	١٠٠٠	أَلْف	alf
10,000	١٠ر٠٠٠	عَشَرَة آلاف	ᶜashara alaaf
1,000,000	١ر٠٠٠ر٠٠٠	مَلْيُون	malyoon
1,000,000,000	١ر٠٠٠ر٠٠٠ر٠٠٠	بَلْيُون	balyoon

(1) To make it simpler, other grammatical rules such as masc. and fem. etc. are avoided at this stage.

THE ORDINAL NUMBERS

English	Arabic masc.	Pronunciation	Arabic Fem.	Pronunciation
the first	الأوّلْ	al-awwal	الأُولَى	al-oolaa
the second	الثَّانى	ath-thanee	الثَّانِيَة	ath-thaaniya
the third	الثَّالِث	ath-thalith	الثَّالِثَة	ath-thalithaa
the fourth	الرَّابِعْ	ar-rabi^c	الرَّابِعَة	ar-rabi^ca
the fifth	الخَامِسْ	al-khamis	الخَامِسَة	al-khamisa
the sixth	السّادِس	as-saadis	السّادِسَة	as-saddisa
the seventh	السّابِعْ	as-sabi^c	السَّابِعَة	as-sabi^ca
the eighth	الثّامِنْ	ath-thamin	الثَّامِنَة	ath-thamina
the ninth	التَّاسِعْ	attaasi^c	التَّاسِعَة	attaasi^ca
the tenth	العَّاشِرْ	al^caashir	العَّاشِرَة	al ^cahsira
the eleventh	الحادِى عَشَرَ	alhaadi ashar	الحَادِيَة عَشَرَة	al hadiya asharata
the 21st	الحادِى والعِشرُونَ	al haadi wal ishroon	الحَادِيَةُ والعِشرُونَ	al hadiya wal ishroon
the 32nd	الثَّانى والثّلاثُونَ	ath-thanee wath-thalaathoon	الثَّانِيَةُ والثَّلاثُونَ	ath-thaaniya wath-thalaath-oon
the 54th etc.	الرابِع والخَمسُون	ar-rabi^cwal khamsoon	الرَّابِعَة والخَمسُونَ	ar-rabi^ca wal kham-soon

FRACTIONS

English	Arabic	Pronunciation
half $^{1}/_{2}$	نُصْف	nusf
one third $^{1}/_{3}$	ثُلْث	thulth
quarter $^{1}/_{4}$	رُبْع	rub^{c}a
one fifth $^{1}/_{5}$	خُمْس	khums
one sixth $^{1}/_{6}$	سُدْس	suds
one seventh $^{1}/_{7}$	سُبْع	sub^{c}a
one eighth $^{1}/_{8}$	ثُمْن	thumn
one ninth $^{1}/_{9}$	تُسْع	tus^{c}
one tenth $^{1}/_{10}$	عُشْر	^{c}ushr

THE VERB

Arabic verbs are mostly triliteral. They are based on roots of three consonants. Thus the basic meaning of writing is given by the three consonants k-t-b (كتب). There are two main tenses: the Perfect (الماضى) al-maḍhee, denoting actions completed at the time to which reference is being made; and the Imperfect (المضارع) al-muḍaari' for incomplete actions. There is also an Imperative الأمر al-amr.

THE PERFECT

(PAST TENSE) الماضى AL-MAḌEE [1]

English	Arabic	Pronunciation
I have written or I wrote	كَتَبْتُ	katabtu
We have written or we wrote	كَتَبْنَا	katabnaa
You (masc) have written or you wrote	كَتَبْتَ	katabta
You (pl / masc) have written or you wrote	كَتَبْتُمْ	katabtum
You (fem) have written or you wrote	كَتَبْتِ	katabti
You (pl / fem) have written or you wrote	كَتَبْتُنَّ	katabtunna
He has written or he wrote	كَتَبَ	kataba
They have written or they wrote	كَتَبُوا	kataboo
She has written or she wrote	كَتَبَتْ	katabat
They have written or they wrote	كَتَبْنَ	katabna

1 - In the conjugation of the past tense dual form is avoided. Learners are advised to learn the conjugation by heart.

THE IMPERFECT

(PRESENT / FUTURE TENSE) المضارع [(1)]

English	Arabic	Pronunciation
I shall write or I write	أَكْتُبُ	aktubu
We shall write or we write	نَكْتُبُ	naktubu
You (masc) will write or you write	تَكْتُبُ	taktubu
You (pl/masc) will write or you write	تَكْتُبُونَ	taktubuna
You (fem) will write or you write	تَكْتُبِينَ	taktubina
You (pl/fem) will write or you write	تَكْتُبْنَ	taktubna
He will write or he writes	يَكْتُبُ	yaktubu
They will write or they write	يَكْتُبُونَ	yaktuboona
She will write or she writes	تَكْتُبُ	taktubu
They will write or they write	يَكْتُبْنَ	yaktubna

(1) Dual form is avoided and learners are again advised to memorise the conjugation.

THE IMPERATIVE (الأمر) (1)

English	Arabic	Pronunciation
You (masc) write	أُكْتُبْ	uktub
You all (masc) write	أُكْتُبُوْا	uktuboo
You (fem) write	أُكْتُبِى	uktubee
You all (fem) write	أُكْتُبْنَ	uktubna

THE NEGATIVE IMPERATIVE (النهى) (2)

English	Arabic	Pronunciation
You (masc) do not write	لا تَكْتُبْ	laa taktub
You all (masc) do not write	لا تَكْتُبُوْا	lal taktuboo
You (fem) do not write	لا تَكْتُبِى	laa taktubee
You all (fem) do not write	لا تَكْتُبْنَ	laa taktubna

(1 & 2) Dual form is avoided.

LIST OF USEFUL VERBS

Instead of mentioning the complicated rules of forming the different tenses, we mention here different forms of the tenses for easy learning.

English	Perfect	Imperfect	Imperative
To be absent	غَابَ ghaaba	يَغِيبُ yagheebu	غِبْ ghib
To absorb	إمْتَصَّ imtaṣṣa	يَمْتَصُّ yamtaṣṣu	إمْتَصْ imtaṣ
To accept	قَبِلَ qabila	يَقْبَلُ yaqbalu	إقْبَلْ iqbal
To acknowledge	إعْتَرَفَ iʿtarafa	يَعْتَرِفُ yaʿtarifu	إعْتَرِفْ iʿtarif
To accompany	رَافَقَ rafaqa	يُرَافِقُ yurafiqu	رَافِقْ rafiq
To advice	نَصَحَ kaṣaha	يَنصَحُ yanṣaḥu	إنْصَحْ inṣaḥ
To be afraid	خَافَ khaafa	يَخَافُ yakhaafu	خَفْ khaf
To agree	اتَّفَقَ (على) ittafaqa	يَتَّفِقُ yattafiqu	اتَّفِقْ ittafiq
To announce	أعْلَنَ aʿlana	يُعْلِنُ yuʿlinu	أعْلِنْ aʿlin
To answer	أجَابَ ajaaba	يُجِيبُ yujeebu	أجِبْ ajib
To appoint	عَيَّنَ ʿaiyana	يُعَيِّنُ yuʿaiyinu	عَيِّنْ ʿaiyin
To arrange	رَتَّبَ rattaba	يُرَتِّبُ yurattibu	رَتِّبْ rattib
To arrive	وَصَلَ waṣala	يَصِلُ yaṣilu	صِلْ ṣil
To ask	سَأَلَ sa'ala	يَسْأَلُ ysa'alu	سَلْ sal

To ask for	طَلَبَ ṭalaba	يَطْلُبُ yaṭlubu	أُطْلُبْ uṭlub
To assist	سَاعَدَ saᶜada	يُسَاعِدُ yusaᶜidu	سَاعِدْ saᶜid
To bargain	سَاوَمَ saawama	يُسَاوِمُ yusaawimu	سَاوِمْ saawim
To be	كَانَ kaana	يَكُوْنُ yakoonu	كُنْ kun
To bear	حَمَلَ ḥamala	يَحْمِلُ yaḥmilu	إِحْمِلْ iḥmil
To become	صَارَ ṣaara	يَصِيْرُ yaṣeeru	صِرْ sir
To begin	إِبْتَدَأَ ibtada'a	يَبْتَدِأُ yabtadi'u	اِبْتَدِأْ ibtadi'
To believe	إِعْتَقَدَ iᶜtaqada	يَعْتَقِدُ yaᶜtaqidu	اعْتَقِدْ iᶜtaqid
To betray	خَانَ khaana	يَخُوْنُ yakhoonu	خُنْ khun
To bind	رَبَطَ rabaṭa	يَرْبُطُ yarbuṭu	أُرْبُطْ urbuṭ
To blame	لَامَ laama	يَلُوْمُ yaloomu	لُمْ lum
To borrow	اسْتَعَارَ istaᶜaara	يَسْتَعِيْرُ yastaᶜeeru	اسْتَعِرْ istaᶜir
To break	كَسَرَ kasara	يَكْسِرُ yaksiru	إِكْسِرْ iksir
To bring	أَحْضَرَ aḥdhara	يُحْضِرُ yuḥḍiru	أَحْضِرْ aḥḍir
To build	بَنَى banaa	يَبْنِى yabnee	إِبْنِ ibne
To bury	دَفَنَ dafana	يَدْفِنُ yadfinu	إِدْفِنْ idfin

To buy	اشْتَرَى ishtara	يَشْتَرِي yashtaree	اشْتَرْ ishtar
To call	دَعَا daᶜaa	يَدْعُو yadᶜoo	أُدْعُ udᶜu
To carry	حَمَلَ ḥamala	يَحْمِلُ yaḥmilu	إِحْمِلْ iḥmil
To catch	قَبَضَ (على) qabaḍa	يَقْبِضُ yaqbiḍu	إِقْبِضْ iqbiḍ
To certify	شَهِدَ shahida	يَشْهَدُ yashhadu	إِشْهَدْ ishhad
To change	غَيَّرَ ghayyara	يُغَيِّرُ yughayyeru	غَيِّرْ ghayyir
To choose	اخْتَارَ ikhtaara	يَخْتَارُ yakhtaaru	اخْتَرْ ikhtar
To clean	نَظَّفَ naẓẓfa	يُنَظِّفُ yunaẓẓifu	نَظِّفْ naẓẓif
To collect	جَمَعَ jamaᶜa	يَجْمَعُ yajmaᶜu	إِجْمَعْ ijmaᶜ
To collide	اصْطَدَمَ iṣṭadama	يَصْطَدِمُ yaṣṭadimu	اصْطَدِمْ iṣṭadim
To come	جَاءَ jaa'a	يَجِيءُ yajee'u	جِيءْ ji'
To come down	نَزَلَ nazala	يَنْزِلُ yanzilu	إِنْزِلْ Inzil
To command	أَمَرَ amara	يَأْمُرُ ya'muru	مُرْ mur
To compensate	عَوَّضَ ᶜawwaḍa	يُعَوِّضُ yuᶜawwiḍu	عَوِّضْ ᶜawwiḍ
To complain	اشْتَكَى ishtaka	يَشْتَكِي yashtaki	اشْتَكِ ishtaki

To confirm	أكّدَ akkada	يُؤكّدُ yuakkidu	أكّدْ akkid
To confiscate	صَادَرَ ṣaadara	يُصَادِرُ yuṣaadiru	صَادِرْ ṣadir
To congratulate	هَنّأَ hanna'a	يُهَنّئُ yuhanni'u	هَنّئْ hanni'
To console	سَلّى sallaa	يُسَلّى yusallee	سَلّ salli
To consult	شَاوَرَ shaawara	يُشَاوِرُ yushawiru	شَاوِرْ shaawir
To continue	اسْتَمَرَّ istamarra	يَسْتَمِرُّ yastamirru	اسْتَمِرْ istamir
To converse	تَكَلّمَ takallama	يَتَكَلّمُ yatakallamu	تَكَلّمْ takallam
To convey	نَقَلَ naqala	يَنْقُلُ yanqulu	أُنْقُلْ unqul
To cook	طَبَخَ ṭaba<u>kh</u>a	يَطْبَخُ yaṭbu<u>kh</u>u	أُطْبُخْ uṭbu<u>kh</u>
To copy	نَسَخَ nasa<u>kh</u>a	يَنْسَخُ yansa<u>kh</u>u	إِنْسَخْ insa<u>kh</u>
To correct	صَحّحَ saḥḥaḥa	يُصَحّحُ yuṣaḥḥiḥu	صَحّحْ ṣaḥḥiḥ
To correspond	رَاسَلَ raasala	يُرَاسِلُ yuraasilu	رَاسِلْ raasil
To count	عَدَّ ʿadda	يَعُدُّ yaʿuddu	عُدَّ ʿudda
To cover	غَطّى ghatta	يُغَطّى yughattee	غَطّ ghatti
To create	خَلَقَ <u>kh</u>alaqa	يَخْلُقُ ya<u>kh</u>luqu	أُخْلُقْ u<u>kh</u>luq
To cultivate	زَرَعَ ẓaraʿa	يَزْرَعُ yaẓraʿu	إِزْرَعْ iẓraʿ

To cross	اِجْتَازَ ijtaaza	يَجْتَازُ yajtaazu	اِجْتَزْ ijtaz
To cut	قَطَعَ qaṭaʿa	يَقْطَعُ yaqṭaʿu	إِقْطَعْ iqṭaʿ
To damage	أَتْلَفَ atlafa	يُتْلِفُ yutlifu	أَتْلِفْ atlif
To dance	رَقَصَ raqaṣa	يَرْقُصُ yarquṣu	أُرْقُصْ urquṣ
To dare	جَرُؤَ jaru'a	يَجْرُؤُ yajru'u	أُجْرُؤْ ujru'
To deceive	غَشَّ ghashsha	يَغُشُّ yaghushshu	غُشَّ ghushsha
To decide	قَرَّرَ qarrara	يُقَرِّرُ yuqarriru	قَرِّرْ qarrir
To defend	دَافَعَ daafaʿa	يُدَافِعُ yudaafiʿu	دَافِعْ daafiʿ
To delay	أَخَّرَ akhkhara	يُوَّخِرُ yuakhkhiru	أَخِّرْ akhkhir
To deliver	سَلَّمَ sallama	يُسَلِّمُ yusallimu	سَلِّمْ sallim
To deny	أَنْكَرَ ankara	يُنْكِرُ unkiru	أَنْكِرْ ankir
To depend	تَوَقَّفَ (عَلى) tawaqqafa	يَتَوَقَّفُ yatawaqqafu	تَوَقَّفْ tawaqqaf
To describe	وَصَفَ waṣafa	يَصِفُ yaṣifu	صِفْ ṣif
To deserve	اِسْتَأْهَلَ ista'hala	يَسْتَأْهَلُ yasta'hilu	اِسْتَأْهِلْ ista'hil
To desire	رَغِبَ raghiba	يَرْغَبُ yarghabu	إِرْغَبْ irghab
To die	مَاتَ maata	يَمُوْتُ yamootu	مُتْ mut

To dig	حَفَرَ ḥafara	يَحْفِرُ yaḥfiru	إِحْفِرْ iḥfir
To digest	هَضَمَ haḍama	يَهْضِمُ yahḍimu	إِهْضِمْ ihḍim
To disappear	غَابَ ghaba	يَغِيبُ yagheebu	غِبْ ghib
To discontinue	انْقَطَعَ inqaṭaᶜa	يَنْقَطِعُ yanqaṭiᶜu	انْقَطِعْ inqaṭiᶜ
To divide	قَسَّمَ qassama	يُقَسِّمُ yuqassimu	قَسِّمْ qassim
To do	فَعَلَ faᶜala	يَفْعَلُ yafᶜalu	إِفْعَلْ ifᶜal
To drink	شَرِبَ shariba	يَشْرَبُ yashrabu	إِشْرَبْ ishrab
To drive	سَاقَ saaqa	يَسُوقُ yasooqu	سُقْ suq
To dwell	سَكَنَ sakana	يَسْكُنُ yaskunu	أُسْكُنْ uskun
To earn	كَسَبَ kasaba	يَكْسِبُ yaksibu	إِكْسِبْ iksib
To eat	اَكَلَ akala	يَأْكُلُ ya'kulu	كُلْ kul
To emigrate	هَاجَرَ haajara	يُهَاجِرُ yuhaajiru	هَاجِرْ haajir
To employ	وَظَّفَ waẓẓafa	يُوَظِّفُ yuwaẓẓifu	وَظِّفْ waẓẓif
To empty	أَفْرَغَ afragha	يُفْرِغُ yufrighu	أَفْرِغْ afrigh
To endeavour	اجْتَهَدَ ijtahada	يَجْتَهِدُ yajtahidu	اجْتَهِدْ ijtahid
To enjoy	تَمَتَّعَ tamattaᶜa	يَتَمَتَّعُ yatamattaᶜu	تَمَتَّعْ tamattaᶜ

To enter	دَخَلَ dakhla	يَدْخُلُ yadkhulu	أُدْخُلْ udkhul
To estimate	قَدَّرَ qaddara	يُقَدِّرُ yuqaddiru	قَدِّرْ qaddir
To examine	امْتَحَنَ imtaḥana	يَمْتَحِنُ yamtaḥinu	امْتَحِنْ imtaḥin
To explain	فَسَّرَ fassara	يُفَسِّرُ yufassiru	فَسِّرْ fassir
To extend	مَدَّدَ maddada	يُمَدِّدُ yumaddidu	مَدِّدْ maddid
To face	وَاجَهَ waajaha	يُوَاجِهُ yuwaajihu	وَاجِهْ wajih
To facilitate	سَهَّلَ sahhala	يُسَهِّلُ yusahhilu	سَهِّلْ sahhil
To fall	سَقَطَ saqaṭa	يَسْقُطُ yasquṭu	أُسْقُطْ usquṭ
To fear	خَافَ khaafa	يَخَافُ yakhaafu	خَفْ khaf
To feed	أَطْعَمَ aṭʿama	يُطْعِمُ yuṭʿimu	أَطْعِمْ aṭʿim
To feel	شَعَرَ shaʿara	يَشْعُرُ yashʿuru	أُشْعُرْ ushʿur
To fill	مَلَأَ mala’a	يَمْلَأُ yamla’u	إِمْلَأْ imla’
To find	وَجَدَ wajada	يَجِدُ yajidu	جِدْ jid
To fly	طَارَ Ṭaara	يَطِيْرُ yaṭeeru	طِرْ ṭir
To follow	تَبِعَ tabiʿa	يَتْبَعُ yatbaʿu	إِتْبَعْ itbaʿ
To forget	نَسِيَ nasiya	يَنْسَى yansaa	إِنْسَ insa

To forgive	سَامَحَ saamaḥa	يُسَامِحُ yusaamḥu	سَامِحْ saamiḥ
To gather	جَمَعَ jamaʿa	يَجْمَعُ yajmaʿu	إجْمَعْ ijmaʿ
To get	نَالَ naala	يَنَالُ yanalu	نَلْ nal
To give	أَعْطَى aʿṭaa	يُعْطِى yuʿtee	أَعْطِ aʿṭi
To go	ذَهَبَ dhahaba	يَذْهَبُ yadhhabu	إذْهَبْ idhhab
To go out	خَرَجَ kharaja	يَخْرُجُ yakhruju	أُخْرُجْ ukhruj
To guarantee	ضَمِنَ ḍamina	يَضْمَنُ yaḍmanu	إضْمَنْ iḍman
To guard	حَرَسَ ḥarasa	يَحْرُسُ yaḥrusu	أُحْرُسْ uḥrus
To guide	أَرْشَدَ arshada	يُرْشِدُ yurshidu	أرْشِدْ arshid
To happen	حَدَثَ ḥadatha	يَحْدُثُ yaḥduthu	أُحْدُثْ uḥduth
To hate	كَرِهَ kariha	يَكْرَهُ yakrahu	إكْرَهْ ikrah
To hear	سَمِعَ samiʿa	يَسْمَعُ yasmaʿu	إسْمَعْ ismaʿ
To help	سَاعَدَ saaʿada	يُسَاعِدُ yusaaʿidu	سَاعِدْ saaʿid
To hide	كَتَمَ katama	يَكْتُمُ yaktumu	أُكْتُمْ uktum
To hit	ضَرَبَ ḍaraba	يَضْرِبُ yaḍribu	إضْرِبْ iḍrib
To hold	مَسَكَ masaka	يَمْسِكُ yamsiku	إمْسِكْ imsik

To honour	شَرَّفَ sharrafa	يُشَرِّفُ yusharrifu	شَرِّفْ sharrif
To hope	رَجَأَ rajaa’	يَرْجُوْ yarjoo	أُرْجُ urju
To hunt	اصْطَادَ iṣtaada	يَصْطَادُ yaṣṭaadu	اصْطَدْ iṣṭad
To improve	حَسَّنَ ḥassana	يُحَسِّنُ yuḥassinu	حَسِّنْ ḥassin
To increase	زَادَ zaada	يَزِيْدُ yazeedu	زِدْ zid
To inform	أَخْبَرَ akhbara	يُخْبِرُ yukhbiru	أَخْبِرْ akhbir
To inquire	اسْتَعْلَمَ istaᶜlama	يَسْتَعْلِمُ yastaᶜlimu	اسْتَعْلِمْ istaᶜlim
To inspect	فَتَّشَ fattasha	يُفَتِّشُ yufattishu	فَتِّشْ fattish
To insult	أَهَانَ ahaana	يُهِيْنُ yuheenu	أَهِنْ ahin
To interpret	تَرْجَمَ tarjama	يُتَرْجِمُ yutarjimu	تَرْجِمْ tarjim
To interview	قَابَلَ qaabala	يُقَابِلُ yuqaabilu	قَابِلْ qaabil
To introduce	عَرَّفَ ᶜarrafa	يُعَرِّفُ yuᶜarrifu	عَرِّفْ ᶜarrif
To invent	اخْتَرَعَ ikhtaraᶜa	يَخْتَرِعُ yakhtariᶜu	اِخْتَرِعْ ikhtariᶜ
To invite	دَعَا daᶜaa	يَدْعُوْ yadᶜuoo	أُدْعُ udᶜu
To join	انْضَمَّ inḍamma	يَنْضَمُّ yanḍmmu	انْضَمِمْ inḍamim
To jump	قَفَزَ qafaza	يَقْفِزُ yaqfizu	إِقْفِزْ iqfiz

To keep	حَفِظَ ḥafiẓa	يَحْفَظُ yaḥfaẓu	إِحْفَظْ iḥfaẓ
To kill	قَتَلَ qatala	يَقْتُلُ yaqtulu	أُقْتُلْ uqtul
To kiss	قَبَّلَ qabbala	يُقَبِّلُ yuqabbilu	قَبِّلْ qabbil
To know	عَرَفَ ᶜarafa	يَعْرِفُ yaᶜrifu	إِعْرِفْ iᶜrif
To laugh	ضَحِكَ ḍaḥika	يَضْحَكُ yaḍḥaku	إِضْحَكْ Iḍḥak
To lay	وَضَعَ waḍaᶜa	يَضَعُ yaḍaᶜu	ضَعْ ḍaᶜ
To lead	قَادَ qaada	يَقُوْدُ yaqoodu	قُدْ qud
To learn	تَعَلَّمَ taᶜallama	يَتَعَلَّمُ yataᶜallamu	تَعَلَّمْ taᶜallam
To leave	تَرَكَ taraka	يَتْرُكُ yatruku	اُتْرُكْ utruk
To lie	كَذَبَ kadhba	يَكْذِبُ yaddhibu	إِكْذِبْ ikdhib
To live	سَكَنَ sakana	يَسْكُنُ yuqfillu	أُسْكُنْ uskun
To lock	أَقْفَلَ aqfala	يُقْفِلُ yuqfilu	أَقْفِلْ aqfil
To look	نَظَرَ naẓara	يَنْظُرُ yanẓuru	أُنْظُرْ unẓur
To lose	خَسِرَ khasira	يَخْسَرُ yakhsaru	إِخْسَرْ ikhsar
To love	أَحَبَّ aḥabba	يُحِبُّ yuḥibbu	أَحْبِبْ aḥbib
To make	صَنَعَ ṣanaᶜa	يَصْنَعُ yasnaᶜu	إِصْنَعْ iṣnaᶜ

To manage	أَدَارَ adaara	يُدِيْرُ yudeeru	أَدِرْ adir
To marry	تَزَوَّجَ tazawwaja	يَتَزَوَّجُ yatazawwaju	تَزَوَّجْ tazawwaj
To meet	لَقِيَ laqiya	يَلْقَى yalqaa	إِلْقَ ilqa
To mention	ذَكَرَ dhakara	يَذْكُرُ yadhkuru	أُذْكُرْ udhkur
To name	سَمَّى Sammaa	يُسَمِّي yusammee	سَمِّ sammi
To need	احْتَاجَ إِلى iḥtaaja	يَحْتَاجُ yaḥtaaju	احْتَجْ iḥtaj
To notice	لاَحَظَ laaḥaẓa	يُلاَحِظُ yulaaḥizu	لاَحِظْ laaḥiẓ
To obey	أَطَاعَ aṭaaʿa	يُطِيْعُ yuṭeeʿu	أَطِعْ aṭiʿ
To omit	حَذَفَ ḥadhafa	يَحْذِفُ yahdhifu	إِحْذِفْ iḥdhif
To open	فَتَحَ fataḥa	يَفْتَحُ yaftaḥu	إِفْتَحْ iftaḥ
To order	أَمَرَ amara	يَأْمُرُ ya'muru	مُرْ mur
To overcome	غَلَبَ ghalaba	يَغْلِبُ yaghlibu	إِغْلِبْ ighlib
To partake	شَارَكَ shaaraka	يُشَارِكُ yushaariku	شَارِكْ shaarik
To pass	مَرَّ بـ marra	يَمُرُّ yamurru	مُرَّ murra
To pay	دَفَعَ dafaʿa	يَدْفَعُ yadfaʿu	إِدْفَعْ idfaʿ
To permit	سَمَحَ Samaḥa	يَسْمَحُ yasmaḥu	إِسْمَحْ ismaḥ

To play	لَعِبَ laᶜiba	يَلْعَبُ yalᶜabu	إلْعَبْ ilᶜab
To please	سَرَّ sarra	يَسُرُّ yasurru	سُرَّ surra
To possess	مَلَكَ malaka	يَمْلِكُ yamliku	إمْلِكْ imlik
To postpone	أَخَّرَ akhkhara	يُؤَخِّرُ yuakhkhiru	أَخِّرْ akhkhir
To prevent	مَنَعَ manaᶜa	يَمْنَعُ yamnaᶜu	إمْنَعْ imnaᶜ
To promise	وَعَدَ waᶜada	يَعِدُ yaᶜidu	عِدْ ᶜid
To pull	سَحَبَ saḥaba	يَسْحَبُ yasḥabu	إسْحَبْ isḥab
To push	دَفَعَ dafaᶜa	يَدْفَعُ yadfaᶜu	إدْفَعْ idfaᶜ
To put	وَضَعَ waḍaᶜa	يَضَعُ yaḍaᶜu	ضَعْ ḍaᶜ
To quarrel	تَشَاجَرَ tashaajara	يَتَشَاجَرُ yatashaajaru	تَشَاجَرْ tashaajar
To quench	أَرْوَى arwa	يُرْوِى yurwi	أَرْوِ arwe
To raid	هَاجَمَ haajama	يُهَاجِمُ yuhaajimu	هَاجِمْ haajim
To raise	رَفَعَ rafaᶜa	يَرْفَعُ yarfaᶜu	إرْفَعْ irfaᶜ
To reach	بَلَغَ balagha	يَبْلُغُ yablughu	أُبْلُغْ ublugh
To read	قَرَأَ qara'a	يَقْرَأُ yaqra'u	إقْرَأْ iqra'
To receive	اِسْتَلَمَ istalama	يَسْتَلِمُ yastalimu	اِسْتَلِمْ istalim

To recommend	أوْصَى بـ awsaa	يُوْصِي yoosee	أوْصِ ausi
To refuse	رَفَضَ rafaḍa	يَرْفُضُ yarfuḍu	أرْفُضْ urfuḍ
To register	سَجَّلَ sajjala	يُسَجِّلُ yusajjilu	سَجِّلْ sajjil
To regret	تَأَسَّفَ ta'assafa	يَتَأَسَّفُ yata'assafu	تَأَسَّفْ ta'assaf
To reject	رَفَضَ rafaḍa	يَرْفُضُ yarfuḍu	أرْفُضْ urfuḍ
To remain	بَقِيَ baqiya	يَبْقَى yabqaa	إبْقَ ibqa
To remember	تَذَكَّرَ tadhakkara	يَتَذَكَّرُ yatadhakkaru	تَذَكَّرْ tadhakkar
To remind	ذَكَّرَ بـ dhakkara	يُذَكِّرُ yudhakkiru	ذَكِّرْ dhakkir
To remove	أزَالَ aẓaala	يُزِيْلُ yuẓeelu	أزِلْ aẓil
To renew	جَدَّدَ jaddada	يُجَدِّدُ yujaddidu	جَدِّدْ jaddid
To repair	صَلَّحَ ṣallaḥa	يُصَلِّحُ yuṣalliḥu	صَلِّحْ ṣalliḥ
To repeat	كَرَّرَ karrara	يُكَرِّرُ yukarriru	كَرِّرْ karrir
To reply	رَدَّ radda	يَرُدُّ yaruddu	رُدَّ rudda
To request	رَجَا rajaa	يَرْجُوْ yarjoo	أرْجُ urju
To reserve	حَجَزَ ḥajaza	يَحْجُزُ yaḥjuzu	أحْجُزْ uḥjuz
To respect	احْتَرَمَ iḥtarama	يَحْتَرِمُ yaḥtarimu	احْتَرِمْ iḥtarim

To rest	اسْتَرَاحَ istaraḥa	يَسْتَرِيْحُ yastareeḥu	اسْتَرِحْ istariḥ
To return	رَجَعَ rajaᶜa	يَرْجِعُ yarjiᶜu	إِرْجِعْ irjiᶜ
To ride	رَكِبَ rakiba	يَرْكَبُ yarkabu	إِرْكَبْ irkab
To rise	نَهَضَ nahaḍa	يَنْهَضُ yanhaḍu	إِنْهَضْ inhaḍ
To rub	مَسَحَ masaḥa	يَمْسَحُ yamsaḥu	إِمْسَحْ imsaḥ
To run	جَرَى jaraa	يَجْرِى yajree	إِجْرِ ijri
To run away	هَرَبَ haraba	يَهْرُبُ yahruba	أُهْرُبْ uhrub
To salute	سَلَّمَ sallama	يُسَلِّمُ yusallimu	سَلِّمْ sallim
To say	قَالَ qaala	يَقُوْلُ yaqoolu	قُلْ qul
To seal	خَتَمَ khatama	يَخْتِمُ yakhtimu	إِخْتِمْ ikhtim
To see	شَافَ ṣhaafa	يَشُوْفُ yaṣhoofu	شُفْ ṣhuf
To sell	بَاعَ baaᶜa	يَبِيْعُ yabeeᶜu	بِعْ biᶜ
To send	أَرْسَلَ arsala	يُرْسِلُ yursilu	أَرْسِلْ arsil
To serve	خَدَمَ khadama	يَخْدُمُ yakhdumu	أُخْدُمْ ukhdum
To shave	حَلَقَ ḥalaqa	يَحْلُقُ yaḥluqu	أُحْلُقْ uḥluq
To shout	صَاحَ ṣaaḥa	يَصِيْحُ yaṣeeḥu	صِحْ ṣiḥ

To show	أَظْهَرَ aẓhara	يُظْهِرُ yuẓhiru	أَظْهِرْ aẓhir
To shut	أَغْلَقَ aghlaqa	يُغْلِقُ yughliqu	أَغْلِقْ aghliq
To sing	غنى ghanna	يُغنى yughanni	غَنِّ ghanni
To sit	جَلَسَ jalasa	يَجْلِسُ yajlisu	إِجْلِسْ ijlis
To sleep	نَامَ naama	يَنَامُ yanaamu	نَمْ nam
To smile	تَبَسَّمَ tabassama	يَتَبَسَّمُ yatabassamu	تَبَسَّمْ tabassam
To smoke	دَخَّنَ dakhkhana	يُدَخِّنُ yudakhkhinu	دَخِّنْ dakhkhin
To speak	تَكَلَّمَ takallama	يَتَكَلَّمُ yatakallamu	تَكَلَّمْ takallam
To spend	أَنْفَقَ anfaqa	يُنْفِقُ yunfiqu	أَنْفِقْ anfiq
To spread	نَشَرَ nashara	يَنْشُرُ yanshuru	أُنْشُرْ unshur
To stand	وَقَفَ waqafa	يَقِفُ yaqifu	قِفْ qif
To steal	سَرَقَ saraqa	يَسْرِقُ yasriqu	إِسْرِقْ isriq
To stop	مَنَعَ manaᶜa	يَمْنَعُ yamnaᶜu	إِمْنَعْ imnaᶜ
To stretch	مَدَّ madda	يَمُدُّ yamuddu	مُدَّ mudda
To succeed	فَازَ faaẓa	يَفُوْزُ yafooẓu	فُزْ fuẓ
To suggest	اقْتَرَحَ iqtaraḥa	يَقْتَرِحُ yaqtariḥu	اقْتَرِحْ iqtariḥ
To swallow	بَلَعَ balaᶜa	يَبْلَعُ yablaᶜa	إِبْلَعْ iblaᶜ

To swim	سَبَحَ sabaḥa	يَسْبَحُ yasbaḥu	إِسْبَحْ isbaḥ
To take	أَخَذَ akhadha	يَأْخُذُ yaa'khudhu	خُذْ khudh
To talk	تَحَدَّثَ taḥaddatha	يَتَحَدَّثُ yataḥaddathu	تَحَدَّثْ taḥaddath
To taste	ذَاقَ dhaaqa	يَذُوقُ yadhooqu	ذُقْ dhuq
To teach	عَلَّمَ ʿallama	يُعَلِّمُ yuʿallimu	عَلِّمْ ʿallim
To tell	قَالَ qaala	يَقُولُ yaqoolu	قُلْ qul
To thank	شَكَرَ Shakara	يَشْكُرُ yashkuru	أُشْكُرْ ushkur
To think	فَكَّرَ fakkara	يُفَكِّرُ yufakkiru	فَكِّرْ fakkir
To throw	رَمَى ramaa	يَرْمِي yarmee	إِرْمِ irmi
To tie	رَبَطَ rabaṭa	يَرْبُطُ yarbuṭu	أُرْبُطْ urbuṭ
To be tired	تَعِبَ taʿiba	يَتْعَبُ yatʿabu	إِتْعَبْ itʿab
To touch	لَمَسَ lamasa	يَلْمِسُ yalmisu	إِلْمِسْ ilmis
To translate	تَرْجَمَ tarjama	يُتَرْجِمُ yutarjimu	تَرْجِمْ tarjim
To travel	سَافَرَ saafara	يُسَافِرُ yusaafiru	سَافِرْ saafir
To treat	عَامَلَ ʿaamala	يُعَامِلُ yuʿaamilu	عَامِلْ ʿaamil
To try	حَاوَلَ ḥaawala	يُحَاوِلُ yuḥaawilu	حَاوِلْ ḥaawil
To understand	فَهِمَ fahima	يَفْهَمُ yafhamu	إِفْهَمْ ifham

To unite	وَحَّدَ waḥḥada	يُوَحِّدُ yuwaḥḥidu	وَحِّدْ waḥḥid
To use	اسْتَعْمَلَ istaᶜmala	يَسْتَعْمِلُ yastaᶜmilu	إِسْتَعْمِلْ istaᶜmil
To vaccinate	طَعَّمَ ṭaᶜᶜama	يُطَعِّمُ yuṭaᶜᶜimu	طَعِّمْ ṭaᶜᶜim
To vary	اختَلَفَ ikhtalafa	يَختَلِفُ yakhtalifu	اختَلِفْ ikhtalif
To visit	زَارَ ẓaara	يَزُورُ yaẓooru	زُرْ ẓur
To vomit	تَقَيَّأَ taqayya'a	يَتَقَيَّأُ yataqayya'	تَقَيَّ taqayya
To wait	انتَظَرَ intaẓara	يَنتَظِرُ yantaẓiru	انتَظِرْ intaẓir
To wake	أَيْقَظَ aiqaẓa	يُوقِظُ yooqiẓu	أَيْقِظْ aiqiẓ
To wake up	اسْتَيْقَظَ istaiqaẓa	يَسْتَيْقِظُ yastaiqiẓu	اسْتَيْقِظْ istaiqiẓ
To walk	مَشَى mashaa	يَمْشِي yamshee	أمْشِ imshi
To want	أَرَادَ araada	يُرِيْدُ yureedu	أَرِدْ arid
To wash	غَسَلَ ghasala	يَغْسِلُ yaghsilu	إِغْسِلْ ighsil
To wear	لَبِسَ labisa	يَلْبَسُ yalbasu	إِلْبَسْ ilbas
To weep	بَكَى bakaa	يَبْكِي yabkee	إِبْكِ ibki
To wish	تَمَنَّى tamannaa	يَتَمَنَّى yatamanna	تَمَنَّ tamanni
To wonder	اسْتَغْرَبَ istaghraba	يَسْتَغْرِبُ yastaghribu	اسْتَغْرِبْ istaghrib
To write	كَتَبَ kataba	يَكْتُبُ yaktubu	أُكْتُبْ uktub

INTRODUCTION
تعارف / TAᶜAARUF

(In the street)

Mr Arif : Hello.	السيد عارف : مَرْحَبًا assayid ᶜaarif : marḥabaa
Mr Samy : Hello.	السيد سامى : مَرْحَبًا assayid Saamee : marḥabaa
Mr Arif : I am Arif.	السيد عارف : أنا عارف assayid ᶜaarif : anaa ᶜaarif
Mr Samy : My name is Samy.	السيد سامى : إسمي سامى assayid saamee : Ismee saamee
Mr Arif : I am an Indian.	السيد عارف : أنا هندي assayid ᶜaarif : anaa ḥindee
I am a businessman.	أنا رجل أعمال anaa rajul aᶜmaal
This is my wife Nabeela.	هذه زوجتي نبيلة hadhehee zaujatee nabeelaa
This is my son Hassan.	وهذا إبني حسن wa ḥaadha ibnee ḥasan
This is my daughter Sameera.	وهذه بنتي سميرة wa haadhehee bintee sameera
Mr Samy: I am an American.	السيد سامى : أنا أمريكي assayid saamee : anaa amreekee
I am a tourist.	أنا سائح anaa saayeḥ
This is my daughter Salma.	وهذه بنتي سلمى wa haadhehee bintee salma
She is a student.	وهى طالبة waheya ṭaleba

(In the University)

Mr Hasan: Good morning.	السيد حسن : صباح الخير assayid hasan : ṣabaahal khair
Miss Salma: Good morning, How are you?	الآنسة سلمى : صباح النور وكيفَ حالك؟ alaanisa Salma : sabaaha-noor wa kaifa ḥaaluk
Mr Hasan: I am well, Thank you. And you?	السيد حسن : أنا بخير شكرا وكيف حالكِ ؟ assayid ḥasan : anaa bekhair, shukran wa kaifa ḥaaluke
Miss Salma: Very well.	الآنسة سلمى : أنا بخير وعافية alaanisa Salma : anaa be khair wa ʿaafiya
Are you Japanese?	هل أنت يابانى ؟ ḥal anta yaabaanee
Mr Hassan: No, I am an Indian.	السيد حسن : لا، أنا هندي assayid ḥasan: laa, anaa hindee
Miss Salma: What do you do?	الآنسة سلمى : ماذا تعمل ؟ alaanisa Salma : maadhaa taʿmal
Mr Hassan: I am a student.	السيد حسن : أنا طالب assayid ḥasan: anaa ṭaalib
Miss Salma: What is your name?	الآنسة سلمى : ما اسمك ؟ alaanisa Salma : masmuk
Mr Hassan: My name is Hassan.	السيد حسن : اسمى حسن assayid ḥasan: ismee ḥasan

Miss Salma: Who is he?	الآنسة سلمى : من هذا ؟ alaanisa Salma: man haadhaa
Mr Hassan: He is my friend.	السيد حسن : هذا صديقي assayid ḥasan: hadhaa Ṣadeeqee
Miss Salma: Which country does he come from?	الآنسة سلمى : من أي بلد هو؟ alaanisa Salma: min ayye balad huwa
Mr Hassan: He is from Canada.	السيد حسن هو من كندا assayid ḥasan: huwa min kanada
Miss Salma: Where do you stay in Baghdad?	الآنسة سلمى : أين تسكن فى بغداد ؟ alaanisa Salma: aina taskuno fi Baghdad?
Mr Hassan: I stay in Al-Rasheed Street.	السيد حسن : أنا أسكن فى شارع الرشيد assayid ḥasan: anaa askunu fee shaareʿ arrasheed
and where do you stay?	وأين أنتِ تسكنين ؟ wa aina ante taskuneena
Miss Salma: I stay in a hotel in Al-Maamoon street.	الآنسة سلمى : أنا أسكن فى فندق فى شارع المامون alaanisa Salma : anaa askunu fee funduq fee ṣhaareʿ almaamoon
Mr Hassan: Goodbye, Miss Salma.	السيد حسن : مع السلامة يا آنسة سلمى assayid ḥasan : maʿassalaama yaa aanisa Salma

Miss Salma: Goodbye, Hassan. الآنسة سلمى : مع السلامة

يا حسن

alaanisa Salma:
ma^{c}assalaama yaa ḥasan

See you tomorrow. سنلتقى بكرة

sanaltaqee bukraa

NOTE :

(1) Arabic is a very rich and meaningful language. It is full of the expressions of blessings and supplication from God, which are usually not found in other languages. For example the word *'marḥaba'* which is generally used for 'Hello' means welcome. The best expression for greeting some one in Arabic is *'As-Salamu alaikum'* which means 'peace be upon you'. It's reply is *'wa alaikumus salam wa raḥmatullah'* (peace and mercy of God be upon you). It means that the reply must be better than the first greeting. The above expression can be used for any person of any age and at any time.

(2) We mention here some expressions for greeting which are originally derived from English and nowadays are commonly used in Arabic.

Good morning.	صباح الخير Ṣabaaḥal khair
Reply:	صباح النور Ṣabaaḥannoor
Good evening.	مساء الخير masaa'al khair
Reply:	مساء النور masaa'annoor
Good day.	نهارك سعيد nahaaruka saᶜeed
Reply:	نهارك أسعد nahaaruka asᶜad
Good night.	تصبحوا على الخير tusbiḥoo ᶜalal khair
Reply:	وأنت من أهل الخير wa anta min ahlel khair
Goodbye.	مع السلامة maᶜassalama
Reply:	مع السلامة إلى اللقاء maᶜassalaama ilalleqaye
Welcome.	أهلاً وسهْلاً ahlan wa sahlan
How do you do?	تشرفنا ! tasharrafna
How are you?	كيف حالك ؟ kaifa ḥaalak
I am fine.	أنا بخير / الحمد لله anaa bekhair / alḥamdulillaah
I am pleased to see you.	أنا سعيد بلقائك anaa saᶜeed beliqayeka

I am happy.	أنا فرحان amaa farḥaan
See you again.	سنلتقى قريبا sanaltaqee qareeban
I wish you all the best.	أتمنى لك كل التوفيق atamanna laka kullattaufeeq
I wish you a happy journey.	أتمنى لك رحلة سعيدة atamanna laka reḥla ṣaʿeeda
Congratulations.	تهانينا / مبروك tahaneena / mabrook

CONTACT / الاتصال

(On telephone) بالتلفون

Mr Hussan: Hello.	السيد حسن : مرحبا assayid ḥasan : marḥabaa
Miss Salma: Hello, what can I do for you?	الآنسة سلمى: مرحبا، أي خدمة؟ alaanisa salma : marḥabaa, ayya khidma
Mr Hassan: Mr Zaid, please.	السيد حسن : رجاءً السيد زيد assayid ḥasan : rajaa'an assayid zaid
Miss Salma: Yes, hold on. He is coming.	الآنسة سلمى : نعم، انتظر رجاءً هو جاءِى alaanisa salma : naʿaam, intazir rajaa'an huwa jaa'ee
Mr zaid: Hellow, how are you Mr Hassan?	السيد زيد : مرحبا، كيف حالك ياسيد حسن ؟ assayid ẓaid: marḥabaa, kaifa ḥaaluk yaa sayid ḥasan
Mr Hassan: I am fine. I am sorry to disturb you.	السيد حسين : الحمد لله، أنا آسف على إزعاجك assayid ḥassa : alḥamdu lillah, anaa aasif ʿalaa izʿaajik
Mr Zaid: Not at all, on the contrary, I thank you for calling.	السيد زيد : كلا، بالعكس، أنا أشكرك للاتصال assayid ẓaid : kallaa, bilʿaks, anaa ashkuruka lil itteṣal
Mr Hassan: How is the family?	السيد حسن : كيف الأهل ؟ assayid ḥasan : kaifal ahl
Mr Zaid: All are hale and hearty.	السيد زيد : كلهم بخير وعافية assayid zaid: kullhum bekhair wa ʿaafiya

ASKING TO MEET SOMEONE

الطلب للقاء شخص ما

I.

Mr Hassan: Excuse me. I am a foreign student and I would like to meet Mr Zaid.	السيد حسن : اسمح لي، أنا طالب أجنبي أود أن أقابل السيد زيد assayid hasan : ismaḥ lee, anaa taalib ajnabi, awaddu an uqaabila assayid zaid
Mr Arif: Sorry, he was here 5 minutes back and he has just left.	السيد عارف : آسف، إنه كان هنا قبل ٥ دقائق وغادر تواً . assayid ʿaarif : aasif, innahu kaana huna qabla khamsa daqaayiq wa ghaadara tauwan
Mr Hassan: When I can meet him ?	السيد حسن : متى يمكنني أن أقابله ؟ assayid hasan : mataa yumkenunee an uqaabilahu
Mr Arif: Tomorrow, he will be in the office at 10 o'clock.	السيد عارف : غدًا، سيكون فى مكتبه فى الساعة العاشرة assayid ʿaarif : ghadan, sayakoonu fee maktabihee fissaaʿa al-ʿaashira
Mr Hassan: Okay, then tomorrow. thank you.	السيد حسن : حسنا، إذا غدًا، شكرا لك assayid hasan : ḥasanan, idhan ghadan, shukran laka
Mr Arif: Welcome.	السيد عارف : يا مرحبا assayid ʿaarif : yaa marhabaa

II.

Mr Hassan: Hello, can I speak to Mr Zaid?	السيد حسن : مرحبا، أريد أن أتكلم مع السيد زيد ؟ assayid ḥasan : marḥabaa, ureedu an atakallama maᶜassyid zaid
Mr Arif: I am sorry. He is not here. Can you call back in 10 minutes?	السيد عارف : أنا آسف، هو غير موجود هنا، هل يمكنك أن تخابر بعد ١٠ دقائق ؟ assayid ᶜaarif : anaa aasif, huwa ghair maujood hunaa. hal yumkenuka an tukhabir baᶜd ashra daqaayek
Mr Hassan: No, it is not possible. Can I leave a message for him?	السيد حسن : لا، إنه غير ممكن، هل يمكنني أن أترك له رسالة ؟ assayid ḥasan: laa, innahu ghair mumkin. hal yumkinunee an atruka lahu resaala
Mr Arif: Of course, I am at your service.	السيد عارف : طبعاً، أنا فى خدمتكم assayid arif: ṭabᶜan anaa fee khidmatikum

INVITATIONS

دعوات

Mr Hassan: I would like you to have lunch with us.	السيد حسن: أنا أود أن تتغدى معنا . assayid ḥasan: anaa awaddu an tataghadda maʿanaa
Mr Arif: I am sorry, I have some work.	السيد عارف : أنا آسف، عندي بعض الشغل . assayid ʿaarif: anaa aasif, ʿndee baʿḍu shshughl
Mr Hassan: Then, please have dinner with us.	السيد حسن : اذا أرجوك أن تتعشى معنا assayid ḥasan: idhan arjooka an tataʿashshaa maʿaana
Mr Arif: You are kind to have thought of me, but I don't want to bother you. You are already four.	السيد عارف : إنك كريم فكّرت عني ولكنني لا أريد إزعاجك، وأنتم الأربعة بالفعل . assayid ʿaarif: innaka kareem, fakkarta ʿannee, walakinnanee laa ureedu izʿaajak, wa antum alarbaʿa bil feʿl
Mr Hassan: You are funny. There is enough food for 5 persons.	السيد حسن: إنك مضحك . الأكل يكفى لخمسة . assayid ḥasan: innaka muḍḥik. alakal yakfee le-khamsa
Mr Arif: Okay, Then I will come.	السيد عارف: حسنا، إذًا سأجئ assayid ʿaarif: ḥasanan, iḍhan saajee.

Note: There are some useful expressions:

Please.	رجاءً / من فَضلِك rajaa'an / min fadlik
Please do.	تفضّلْ tafaḍḍal
Thank you.	شكرًا shukran
Reply: Not at all.	عفوًا ʿafwan
Thanks a lot.	ألف شكر alf shukr
I am very grateful.	أنا ممنون جدًا anaa mamnoon jiddan
Reply: Don't mention it.	العفوَ alafwa
Do not bother.	لاتقلق laa taqlaq
Sorry, I am busy.	آسف، أنا مشغولْ aasif, anaa mashghool
Excuse me.	اسمح لي ismaḥ lee
Please come in (*masc.*).	تفضّلْ tafaḍḍal
Please come in (*fem.*).	تفضّلى tafaḍḍalee

Note: This expression can be used in any circumstance where a second person is required to do any thing. For example: please sit down, please speak, please eat, etc.

Telephone	تلفون / هاتف telfoon / haatif
Telephone directory	دليل الهاتف daleelul haatif
Receiver	سمّاعة samma^ca
Number	رقم raqm
call	مكالمة / مكالمات mukaalama / mukaalamaat
Local call	مكالمة محلية mukaalama maḥalleeya
Long distance call	مكالمة خارجية mukaalama kharjeeya
Telephone operator	مشغل التلفون mushaghghil-u-ttelefoon
Extension Number	رقم تحويلة raqm taḥweela

HEALTH

الصحة

Mr Hassan: Where is the hospital?	السيد حسن : أين المستشفى؟ assayid ḥasan: aina almustashfaa
Mr Arif: What type of hospital?	السيد عارف: أي نوع من المستشفى؟ assayid ʿaarif: ayya nauʿ minal mustashfaa
Mr Hasan: General hospital.	السيد حسن : مستشفى عام assayid ḥasan: mustashfaa ʿaam
Mr Arif: The general hospital is at Rasheed Street.	السيد عارف: المستشفى العام في شارع الرشيد assayid ʿaarif: almustashfaa alʿaam fee shaareʿ arrasheed
Mr Hasan: How far is it from here?	السيد حسن : كم كيلوميتر من هنا ؟ assayid ḥasan: kam kilomeetar min hunaa
Mr Arif: Nearly 5 km.	السيد عارف: حوالى ٥ كيلومترات assayid ʿaarif: ḥawalai khamsa kilomitraat
Mr Hasan: How many Deptts are there?	السيد حسن : كم قسما فيه ؟ assayid ḥasan: kam qisman feehe

Mr Arif: That is a big hospital. You will find there all the facilities, like X-ray, pharmacy, etc.	السيد عارف : ذالك مستشفى كبير ، ستجد فيه كل التسهيلات أمثال الأشعة، و الصيدلة وغيرها .
	assayid ʿaarif: dhaalika mustashfaa kabeer, satajid feehe kulla ttasheelaat amthaal alasheʿʿa wa ṣṣaidala wa ghairahaa

USEFUL VOCABULARIES
مفردات مفيدة

Clinic	عيادة ʿiyaada
Indoor patient	عيادة داخلية ʿiyaada daakhleeya
Outdoor patient	عيادة خارجية ʿiyaada kharjeeya
X-ray	الأشعة alasheʿʿa
Doctor	طبيب ṭabeeb
Nurse	ممرّضة mumarrida
Specialist	إخصائي ikhṣayee
Check up	فحص faḥaṣ
Report	تقرير taqreer
Prescription	وصفة طبية waṣfa ṭibbeeya
Patient	مريض mareeḍ
Disease	مرض maraḍ
Pain	ألم / وجع alam/wajaʿ
Treatment	علاج ʿilaaj
Blood	دم dam
Fracture	كسر kasr
Cut	قطع qaṭʿ
Toothache	وجع فى السن wajaʿ fissin
Stomach ache	وجع فى البطن wajaʿ fil batn
Headache	صُداع ṣudaaʿ
Cold	برد bard
Cough	كحه / سعال kuḥḥa / suʿaal
Fever	حمى ḥummaa
Typhoid	حمى معوية ḥummaa miʿweeya

VISIT TO DOCTOR

زيارة للطبيب

Mr Hassan: Good morning doctor.	السيد حسن : صباح الخير يا طبيب. assayid ḥasan: ṣabaaḥal khair yaa ṭabeeb
Doctor: Good morning. Hassan. So what brings you here ?	الطبيب : صباح النور يا حسن ما الذى جاء بك هنا ؟ aṭṭabeeb: ṣabaaḥannoor yaa Ḥasan, malladhee jaaʿa bika hunaa
Mr Hassan: I am suffering from fever and severe cough.	السيد حسن : أنا مصاب بحمى وكحة شديدة. assayid ḥasan:anaa muṣaab biḥumma wa kuḥha shadeeda
Doctor: Do you smoke?	الطبيب : هل تدخن؟ attabeeb: hal tudakhkhin
Mr Hassan: No.	السيد حسن : لا assayid ḥasan: Laa
Doctor: Take this medicine from the pharmacy.	الطبيب : خذ هذا الدواء من الصيدلة attabeeb: khudh ḥaadha ddawa mina ṣṣaidala
Mr Hassan: How shall I take it?	السيد حسن : كيف آخذه ؟ assayid ḥasan: kaifa aakhudhuhu
Doctor:. One spoonful every four hours.	الطبيب : ملعقة كل أربع ساعات aṭṭabeeb: milʿaqa kulla arbaʿa saaʿaat
Mr Hassan: For how many days?	السيد حسن : لمدة كم يوم؟ assayid ḥasan: limudda kam yaum

Doctor: Four days. | الطبيب : أربعة أيام
aṭṭbeeb: arbaʿa ayyaam

Mr Hassan: Where is the pharmacy? | السيد حسن : أين الصيدلة ؟
assayid ḥasan: aina ṣṣaidala

Doctor: Behind this building. | الطبيب : خلف هذا المبنى
aṭṭbeeb: khalfa haadhal mabna

Mr Hassan: Do you have this medicine? | السيد حسن : هل عندك هذا الدواء ؟
assayid ḥasan: hal ʿindaka haadhaddawa

Chemist: Yes. | الصيدلي : نعم
aṣṣaidalee: naʿam

Mr Hassan: How much does this medicine cost? | السيد حسن : ما ثمن هذا الدواء؟
assayid ḥasan: maa thamanu haadhaaddawa

Chemist: Rs. 10 only. | الصيدلي : عشر روبيات فقط
aṣṣaidalee: ashara roobeyaat faqat

Mr Hassan: Thanks. | السيد حسن : شكرا
assayid ḥasan: shukran

USEFUL VOCABULARIES
مفردات مفيدة

Bed	سرير sareer
Injection	حقنة ḥuqna
Tetanus injection	حقنة ضد الكُزّاز ḥuqna diddal kuzzaz
Pills	حبوب ḥuboob
Capsule	كبسولة kabsoola
Syringe	مِحقنة miḥqana
Syrup	شراب sharaab
Solution	دواء محلول dawa maḥlool
Blood sample	عينة الدم ʿaiyanatuddam
Urine sample	عينة البول ʿaiyanatul baul
operation	عملية جراحية ʿamaleeya jeraaheeya
Blood pressure	ضغط الدم ḍaghtuddam
Accident	حادث ḥadith
Road accident	حادث السيارة ḥaadithussaiyara
Injury	إصابة ḥaadith
Head injury	إصابة بالرأس iṣaaba birras
Orthopedics	تجبير العظام jajbeerul ʿizaam
Surgery	جراحة jiraaḥa
Dental surgery	جراحة الأسنان jiraaḥatul asnaan
Surgeon	طبيب جرّاح ṭabeeb jarrah

Heart specialist	إخصائي القلب ikhṣaayee-u-lqalb
Eye specialist	إخصائي العيون ikhsaayee-ul-ᶜuyoon
Sick	مريض mareeḍ
Temperature	درجة حرارة daraja ḥaraara
Condition	حالة ᶜhala
Good	جيد jayyid
Bad	ردئ radee
Chest	صدر ṣadr
Leg	رجل rijl
Throat	حلق ḥalaq
Mouth	فم fam
Inflammation	التهاب iltihaab
Stomach	معدة maᶜida

THE POST OFFICE

مكتب البريد / maktabul bareed

Mr Hassan: Is that the post office?	السيد حسن : هل ذلك مكتب البريد ؟ assayid ḥasan: hal dhalika maktabul bareed
Mr Arif: No, the post office is in-front of the railway station.	السيد عارف: لا، مكتب البريد أمام محطة القطار . assayid ʿaarif: laa, maktabul bareed amaama maḥattatil qitaar
Mr Hassan: Thank you.	السيد حسن : شكرا . assayid ḥasan: shukran
Mr Hassan: Sir, I am a foreigner and I want to send a telegram.	السيد حسن : سيدي، أنا أجنبي وأنا أريد إرسال برقية . assayid ḥasan: sayyedee, anaa ajnabee wa anaa ureedu irsal barqeyya
Post Office Man: Please fill this form.	موظف البريد : رجاءً إملأ هذه الاستمارة . muwaẓẓaful bareed: rajaa'an, imla' ḥaadhihil istammara
Mr Hassan: Is it okay?	السيد حسن : هل هذا مضبوط؟ assayid ḥasan: hal haadhaa maḍboot
Post Office man: The name of addressee is not clear.	موظف البريد : إسم المرسل إليه غير واضح . muwaẓẓaful bareed: ismul mursal ilaihe ghair waḍeh

Mr Hassan: His name is Arif.	السيد حسن : إسمه عارف . assayid ḥasan: ismuhu ᶜaarif
Post Office man: Is it urgent or ordinary?	موظف البريد : هل هذه البرقية مستعجلة أو عادية ؟ muwaẓẓaful bareed: hal haadhihil barqiyya mustaᶜjila aw ᶜaadiyya
Mr Hassan: Urgent.	السيد حسن : مستعجل . assayid ḥasan: mustaᶜjal
Post Office man: Please pay Rs 20.	موظف البريد : رجاءً إدفع عشرين روبية . muwa ẓẓaful bareed: rajaa'an idfaᶜ ishreen roobiya
Mr Hassan : Please take it.	السيد حسن : رجاءً خذها . assayid ḥasan: rajaa'an khudh haa
Post Office man: Here is the receipt. Any thing else ?	مؤظف البريد : هذا هو الإيصال وأي شئ آخر ؟ muwaẓẓaful bareed: haaḍhaa hual yeeṣal wa ayya shai aakhar
Mr Hassan: Thank you.	السيد حسن : شكرا . assayid ḥasann: shukran

USEFUL VOCABULARY

مفردات مفيدة

Post Office	مكتب البريد maktabul bareed
Ordinary mail	البريد العادي albareed alʿaadee
Air mail	البريد الجوي albareed aljawwee
Express mail	البريد المستعجل albareed almustaʿjal
Registered mail	البريد المسجل albareed almusajjal
Speed post	البريد السريع albareed assareeʿ
Counter	شباك shubbak
Stamp	طابع / طوابع ṭabeʿ
Envelope	ظرف ẓarf
Letters	خطاب / رسالة khiṭab / risaala
Letter box	صندوق البريد ṣundooqul bareed
Post Office stamp	ختم مكتب البريد khatmu maktabil bareed
Parcel	طرد / طرود ṭard
Money order	حوالة بريدية ḥawala bareedeeya
Sender	المرسل almursil
Addressee	المرسل إليه almursal ilaihe

Receipt	إيصال yeeṣal
E- mail	البريد الإلكتروني albareed alelectroonee
Telegram	برقية barqiyya
Card	بطاقة beṭaaqa
Postman	ساعى البريد saʿil bareed

SHOPPING

التسوق / attasawwuq

Mr Hassan: Where are you going?	السيد حسن : أين أنت تذهب؟ assayid ḥasan: aina anta tadhhab
Mr Arif: I am going to the market.	السيد عارف : أنا أذهب إلى السوق . assayid ʿaarif : anaa adhhab ilassoq
Mr Hassan: What will you buy?	السيد حسن : ماذا ستشترى؟ assayid ḥasan: maadhaa satashtaree
Mr Arif: I will buy bread, sugar and clothes.	السيد عارف : سأشترى خبز وسكر وملابس . assayid ʿaarif: saashtaree khubz wa sukkar wa malaabis
(Mr Arif in clothes shop)	(السيد عارف فى محل الملابس) assayid ʿaarif fee mahallil malaabis
Mr Arif: I want to buy a shirt.	السيد عارف : أريد أن أشترى قميصا . assayid ʿaarif: ureedu an ashtaree qameeṣ
Salesman: I have a beautiful collection.	البائع : عندي مجموعات جميلة. albaa'ʿ: ʿindee majmooʿaat jameelaa
Mr Arif: What kind of material is this?	السيد عارف : ما صنف هذا القماش؟ assayid ʿaarif: maa ṣinfu haadhal qumaash

Salesman: It is silk.	البائع : هذا القماش حرير . albaa'eʿ: haadhal qumash ḥareer
Mr Arif: What size is this shirt?	السيد عارف: ما مقاس هذا القميص؟ assayid ʿaarif: maa maqasu haadhal qameeṣ
Salesman: It is medium.	البائع : مقاسه متوسط albaa'eʿ: maqaasuhu mutawassit
Mr Arif: Do you have a large size?	السيد عارف : هل عندك مقاس أكبر ؟ assayid ʿaarif: hal ʿindaka maqaas akbar
Salesman: Yes. this is the large size and this will fit you.	البائع : نعم . هذا المقاس أكبر ، وسوف يناسبكَ . albaa'eʿ: naʿam haadhal mqaasu akbar wa saufa yunasibuka.
Mr Arif: What is the price?	السيد عارف: كم ثمنه؟ assayid ʿaarif: kam thamanuhu
Salesman: 8 dinars only.	البائع : ٨ دنانير فقط . albaa'eʿ: thamaniya danaaneer faqat
Mr Arif: Give me a pair of trousers also, please.	السيد عارف : أعطني بنطلون أيضا، من فضلك . assayid ʿaarif: aʿtenee bantaloon aidhan min fadhlik
Salesman: Do you like this?	البائع : هل يُعْجِبُكَ هذا ؟ albaa'eʿ: hal yuʿjibuka haadhaa

Mr Arif : Well, I shall take it. — السيد عارف : حسنا، آخذه .
assayid ʿaarif: ḥasanan aakhudhuhu

Salesman: Thank you. — البائع : شكرا .
albaa'eʿ: shukran

USEFUL VOCABULARIES

مفردات مفيدة

What is the price of this? — كم ثمن هذا؟
kam thamanu haadhaa

It is cheap. — هذا رخيص .
hadhaa rakhees

It is costly. — هذا غالي .
haadhaa ghaalee

I want........... — أنا أريد
anaa ureed

I do not want............... — أنا لا أريد
anaa laa ureed

Do you have — هل عندك........
hal ʿindaka

Sorry. I do not have — آسف . ليس عندي
aasif laisa ʿindi

Grocer — بقال baqqal

Fruit seller — فاكهاني fakhaanee

Butcher — جزار jazzaar

Baker — خباز khabbaaz

Green grocer — خضري khaḍaree

Florist	زهار ẓahhaar
Barber	حلاق ḥallaaq
Tooth brush	فرشاة الأسنان furshaatul asnaan
Tooth paste	معجون الأسنان maᶜjoonul asnaan
Shaving cream	معجون الحلاقة maᶜajoonul ḥilaaqaa
Shaving blade	شفرة الحلاقة shafaratul ḥilaaqaa
Shaver	آلة الحلاقة الكهربائية aalatul ḥilaaqa alkahrabaayeea
Bread	خبز khubz
Butter	زبدة ẓubda
Jam	مربى murabba
Fruit	فاكهة faakiha
Biscuit	بسكويت biskuwait
Cheese	جبنة jubna
Soap	صابون ṣaaboon
Towel	مِنشفة minshafa
Handkerchief	منديل mindeel
Shoes	حذاء ḥidhaa
Belt	حزام ḥizaam
Perfume	عطر iṭr
Underwears	ملابس داخلية malaabis daakhiliyya

Battery cell	بطارية battaareeya
Bag	حقيبة ḥaqeeba
Rate	سِعر siʿr
Value	قيمة qeema
payment	دَفْع dafʿ
Goods	بَضَائع baḍaa'iʿ
Agent	وكيل wakeel
Agency	وكالة wakaala
Sales	تنزيلات tanzeelaat
Profit	رِبْح ribḥ
Loss	خسارة khasaara
Commission	عمولة ʿamoola

TRAVELLING

السفر / assafar

Tourist: Hello.	السائح : مرحبا assaa'eh: marḥabaa
Officer: Hello, what can I do for you?	الموظف: مرحبا، أي خدمة ؟ almuwaẓẓaf: marhabaa, ayya khidma.
Tourist: I want to visit Arab countries, can you guide me to the important places?	السائح: أريد أن أزور البلدان العربية، أرجوك أن تدلنى على الأماكن الهامة ؟ assaa'eh: ureedu an azoora albuldaan alʿarbiyya, arjooka an tadullanee ʿalal amaakin alhamma.
Officer: Are you an American?	الموظف: هل أنت أمريكي؟ almuwaẓẓaf: hal anta amreekee?
Tourist: No, I am an Indian.	السائح: لا، أنا هندي . assaa'eh: laa, ana hindee
Officer: You can visit Egypt, Iraq and Syria.	الموظف: يمكنك أن تزور مصر والعراق وسورية. almuwaẓẓaf: yumkenuka an tazoora miṣr walʿiraaq wa sooriya
Tourist: Do you have tourist guide?	السائح: هل عندك دليل السياحة؟ assaa'eh: hal ʿindaka daleelussiyaha
Officer: You can get it at the airport.	الموظف: من الممكن أن تجده بالمطار . almuwaẓẓaf: minal mumkin 'an tajidahu bilmaṭaar

Tourist: I want to make a call to No. 6946183.	السائح: أريد مكالمة تلفونية مع رقم ٦٩٤٦١٨٣ assaa'eh: ureedu mukaalama telfooniyya ma^craqm 6946183
Officer: You must wait about 15 minutes.	الموظف: يجب أن تنتظر ربع ساعة . almuwaẓẓaf: yajibu an tantaẓir rub^ca saa^ca
Tourist: Incredible! 15 minutes!	! السائح: يا سلام! ربع ساعة assa'eh : yaa salaam! rub^ca saa^ca
Officer: Where is your luggage?	الموظف: أين عفشك ؟ almuwaẓẓaf: aina ^cafashuka
Tourist: I have only this bag.	السائح: عندي هذه الحقيبة فقط . assa'eh : ^cindee haadhiḥil haqeeba faqat.

USEFUL VOCABULARIES

مفردات مفيدة

Taxi	تاكسى taaksee
Wait	انتظار intizaar
Waiting room	غرفة الانتظار ghurfatul intizaar
Road	طريق ṭareeq
Bridge	جسر jisr
Car	سيارة sayyaara

Driver	سائق saa'eq
Ticket	تذكرة tadḥkira
Seat	مقعد maqʿad
Arrival	وصول wusool
Departure	مغادرة mughaadara
Traffic light	إشارة المرور ishaaratul muroor
Petrol station	محطة البنزين maḥattatul benzeen

AIRPORT

المطار / almaṭaar

Mr Hassan: I am Hassan.	السيد حسن: أنا حسن . assayid ḥasan: anaa hasan
I am a businessman.	أنا رجل أعمال . anaa rajul aʿmaal
I am from Delhi.	أنا من دلهى . anaa min delhee
I am going to London on a business trip.	أنا ذاهب إلى لندن فى رحلة تجارية . anaa dhaahib ila landon fee rehla tijaariyya
Immigration Officer: Which country do you belong to?	ضابط الجوازات والهجرة : من أيِّ بلد أنت؟ ḍaabitul jawaaẓaat wal hijra: min ayye balad anta.
Mr Hassan: I am from India.	السيد حسن: أنا من الهند assayid ḥasan: anaa minal hind
Officer: Where is your passport?	ضابط الجوازات: أين جواز سفرك ؟ ḍaabitul jawaazaat : aina jawaazu safarika
Do you have visa for England?	هل عندك تأشيرة لإنجلترا ؟ hal ʿindaka taasheera leinjaltara
Mr Hassan: Yes.	السيد حسن : نعم assayid ḥasan: naʿam
Officer: At first pay the airport tax.	ضابط الجوازات: أولا إدفع رسوم المطار . ḍaabitul jawaazaat: awwalan idfaʿ rusoomal maṭaar

Mr Hassan: Any other formality?	السيد حسن: أي إجراءات أخرى؟ assayid ḥasan: Ayya ijraa'aat ukhraa
Officer: Then, get the boarding card.	ضابط الجوازات: ثم احصل على بطاقة الركوب ḍaabitul jawaazaat : thumma uḥsul ʿalaa biṭaaqatirrukoob.
Mr Hassan: Where do I handover the baggage?	السيد حسن: أين أسلِّم العفش ؟ assayid ḥasan: aina usallim alʿafash
Officer: To that counter.	ضابط الجوازات: إلى ذالك الشباك . ḍaabitul jawaazaat : ilaa dhalika shshubbaak
Mr Hassan: Where is the duty free shop?	السيد حسن: أين السوق الحرة؟ assayid ḥasan: aina assooq alḥurra
Officer: Near the waiting room.	ضابط الجوازات: قرب صالة الانتظار. ḍaabitul jawaazaat: qurba saalatil intizaar
Mr Hassan: What I have to do at my arrival in England?	السيد حسن: ما عليّ أن أعمل لدى وصولى إلى لندن/إنجلترا؟ assayid ḥasan: maa ʿalayya an aʿmala lada wusoolee ilaa London/injaltaraa

Officer: If you have any foreign goods declare them at the custom. I wish you a happy journey.	ضابط الجوازات: إذا كان معك أشياء أجنبية، صرِّح بذلك لدى الجمرك. أتمنى لك سفرًا سعيدًا ḍaabitul jawaazaat : idhaa kaana maᶜaka ashyaa ajnabiyya, ṣarreḥ bidhaalika ladal jumruk. atamanna laka safaran saᶜeedan
Mr Hassan: Thank you for the help.	السيد حسن : أشكرك على المساعدة assayid ḥasan: ashkuruka ᶜalal musaaᶜada.
Officer: It's alright.	ضابط الجوازات: العفو ḍaabitul jawaazaat: alᶜafw

USEFUL VOCABULARIES

مفردات مفيدة

Arrival	وصول wusool
Departure	مغادِرَة mughaadara
Flight No.	رحلة رقم rehlaa raqm
Airways	الخطوط الجوية alkhuṭooṭ aljawwiyya
Indian airways	الخطوط الجوية الهندية alkhuṭooṭ aljawwiyya alhindiyya
Airport staff	هيئة المطار hai'atul maṭaar
Security staff	رجال الأمن rejaalul amn

Security check up	التفتيش الأمني attafteesh alamnee
Airport Security	إجراءات أمنية فى المطار ijraa'aat amaniyya fil maṭaar
Trolley	عربة نقل ʿarabatu naql
Exchange counter	شباك صرف العملة الأجنبية shubbaaku ṣarfil ʿumla alajnabiyya
Airways offices	مكاتب الطيران makaatibu ṭṭayaran
Customs	الجمرك aljumruk
Custom officer	مفتش الجمرك
Custom rules	قوانين الجمرك qawaaneenul jumruk
Declaration	تصريح المواد الجمركية taṣreeḥul mawaad aljumrukiyya
Custom fine	غرامة جمركية gharama jumrukiyya
Porter	شيال shayyal
Liquor	خمور khumoor
Drugs	مخدرات mukhaddiraat
No Smoking	ممنوع التدخين mamnooʿuttadkheen
No Entry	ممنوع الدخول mamnooʿuddukhool
Smuggling	تهريب tahreeb
Smuggler	مهرب muharrib

Baggage check up	تفتيش الحقائب tafteeshul ḥaqaa'eb
Complaint	شكوى shakwa
Visa	تأشيرة taasheera
Entry visa	تأشيرة الدخول taasheeratuddukhool
Exit visa	تأشيرة الخروج taasheeratul khurooj
Exit and Re-entry visa	تأشيرة الخروج والدخول taasheeratul khurooj waddukhool تأشيرة المغادرة والعودة taasheeratul mughaadara walʿauda
Tourist visa	تأشيرة سياحية taasheera siyaaḥiyya
Visit visa	تأشيرة زيارة taasheeratu ziyara
Work visa	تأشيرة عمل tasheeratu ʿamal
Stamping of passport	ختم جواز السفر khatamu jawazissafar
Ticket	تذكرة tadhkira
To and Fro ticket	تذكرة ذهاب وإياب tadhkiratu dhahaab wa iyaab
Confiscation	مصادرة muṣaadara
Transit visa	تأشيرة المرور taasheeratul muroor

Direct flight	رحلة مباشرة riḥla mubaashira
Take off time	موعد إقلاع mauᶜidu iqlaaᶜ
Landing time	موعد هبوط mauᶜidu huboot
Runway	مدرج الطائرة madrajuṭṭaayera
Crew	طاقم الطائرة ṭaaqimuttaayera
Air hostess	مضيفة mudeefa
Hijacking of plane	اختطاف الطائرة ikhtitaafut taayera
Permanent	دائم daayem
Temporary	مؤقت muwaqqat
Passport	جواز السفر jawazussafar
Passport holder	حامل جواز السفر ḥaamilu jawaazissafar
Nationality	جنسية jinsiyya
Custom duty	رسوم جمركية rusoom jumrukiyya

RAILWAY STATION

محطة القطار / maḥaṭṭatul qiṭaar

This is the Delhi railway station.	هذه محطة قطار دلهى ḥaadhihee maḥaṭṭatu qiṭaar delhee
It is a big station. It has many platforms and many windows for first class, second class and third class tickets.	هى محطة كبيرة وبداخلها أرصفة كثيرة، وشبابيك كثيرة لتذاكر الدرجة الأولى والدرجة الثانية والدرجة الثالثة . hiya maḥṭṭa kabeera wa bedaakhilihaa arṣefa katheera, wa shabaabeek katheera le tadhaakerid daraja al'oola waddaraja aththaaniyya waddaraja aththaaletha
There are many facilities like, a big restaurant, waiting room and P. C. O's offices.	توجد فيها تسهيلات كثيرة أمثال مطعم كبير وصالة الانتظار ومراكز الاتصال الداخلي والخارجي . toojad feehaa tasheelaat katheera amthaal maṭʿam kabeer wa ṣaalatul intizaar wa marakizil ittiṣaal addakhilee wal kharijee
There is a taxi stand and hotel in front of the station.	أمام المحطة يوجد موقف لسيارات الأجرة والفندق . amaamal maḥaṭṭa yojad mauqif lesayyaaraatil ujra wal funduq
This station is always crowded with passengers.	هذه المحطة مزدحمة دائما بالمسافرين . haadhihil maḥaṭṭaa muzdahema daayeman bilmusaafereen

Mr Hassan: My family and I would like to travel to Bombay.	السيد حسن : أريد أن أسافر أنا وأسرتيَ إلى بومباى	assayid ḥasan: Ureedu an usaafira anaa wa usratee ilaa boombaaye.
Enquiry office: By which train?	مكتب الاستعلام : بأي قطار؟	maktabul isteˤlaam: be ayye qiṭaar
Mr Hassan: I do not know. Please suggest some suitable train.	السيد حسن : أنا لا أعرف، أرجوك أن تقترح عليّ بعض القطار المناسب .	assayid ḥasan: anaa laa aˤrif arjooka an taqtareḥ alayya baˤḍal qiṭaar almunaasib
Enquiry office: There are many trains, some passengers and other express.	مكتب الاستعلام : هناك قطارات كثيرة بعضها عادية وأخرى سريعة .	maktabul isteˤlaam: hunaka qiṭaaraat katheera baˤḍuhaa ˤaadiyya, wa ukhraa sareeˤa
Mr Hassan: I will prefer to travel by express train.	السيد حسن : أفضل أن أسافر بالقطار السريع	assayid ḥasan: ufaddilu an usaafera bil qiṭaar assareeˤ
Enquiry office: Then you take Rajdhani train No. 5224 which leaves at 7:00 p.m.	مكتب الاستعلام : إذاً خذ قطار راجدهانى رقم ٥٢٢٤ الذى يغادر فىالساعة السابعة مساءً	maktabul isteˤlaam: idhan khudh qitaar raajdhanee raqm 5224 alladhee yughaadiru fissaaˤa assaabiˤa masaa'an

Mr Hassan: When will it reach Bombay?	السيد حسن : متى سيصل إلى بومباى؟ assayid ḥasan: maṭa sayaṣil ilaa boombaaye
Enquiry office: Next day morning at 9:00 a.m.	مكتب الاستعلام : صباح اليوم التالي في الساعة التاسعة . maktabul isteʿlaam: ṣabaahal yaum attaalee fissaaʿa attaaseʿa
Mr Hassan: Where can I buy the ticket?	السيد حسن : من أين يمكننى أن أشترى تذكرة ؟ assayid ḥasan: min aina yumkenunee an ashtaree tadhkera.
Enquiry office: From counter no. 125.	مكتب الاستعلام : من شباك رقم ١٢٥ . maktabul isteʿlaam: min shubbak raqm 125
Mr Hassan: I want three tickets of Rajdhani for Bombay.	السيد حسن : أريد ثلاث تذاكر لبومباى لقطار راجدهانى . assayid ḥasan: ureedu thalaatha tadhaakir le boombaaye leqiṭaar raajdhaanee
Officer : Rs 3,000 please.	الموظف : ثلاثة آلاف روبية من فضلك . almuwaẓẓaf: thalaatha aalaaf roobiya min faḍlik
Mr Hassan: Give me first class A.C. tickets.	السيد حسن : أعطنى تذكرة الدرجة الأولى المكيفة الهواء . assayid ḥasan: aʿtenee tadhkirataddaraja al'oolaa almukayyifatil hawa

Officer : Then you pay Rs 9000/-

المؤظف : إذاً إدفع تسعة آلاف روبية .

almuwaẓẓaf: idhan idfaᶜ tisᶜa aalaaf rubiya

Mr Hassan: Thank you.

السيد حسن : شكرًا .

assayid ḥasan: shukran

Officer : Not at all.

المؤظف : العفو .

almuwaẓẓaf: alafwa

USEFUL VOCABULARIES

مفردات مفيدة

Porter	شيال shayyaal
Enquiry office	مكتب الاستعلام maktabul isteᶜlaam
Platform ticket	تذكرة الرصيف tadhkiraturraṣeef
Return ticket	تذكرة العودة tadhkiratulᶜauda
Sleeper coach	عربة النوم ᶜarabatunnaum
Dining car	عربة الأكل ᶜarabatul akl
Freight car	عربة الشحن ᶜarabatushshaḥan
Reservation office	مكتب الحجز maktabul hajẓ
Left luggage office	مكتب الأمانات maktabul amaanaat
Receive	استقبال isteqbaal
See off	توديع taudeeᶜ
Entry	الدخول addukhool

Exit	الخروج alkhorooj
Toilet	مرافق maraafiq
In time	فيّ الميعاد fil meeʿaad
Late	متأخر muta-akhkhir
Comfortable	مريح mureeḥ
Uncomfortable	غير مريح ghair mureeḥ
Soft drink	المشروبات الغازية almashroobaat alghaaziyya
Tea	شاي shaae
Coffee	قهوة qahwa
Cigarette	سيجارة seejaara
To wait	انتظار intizaar
Direct train	قطار مباشر qitaar mubaashir

BANK / البنك

Mr Hassan: Good morning!	السيد حسن : صباح الخير ! assayid ḥasan: ṣabaaḥal khair
Bank clerk: Good morning! what can I do for you?	الموظف : صباح النور ! أي خدمة ؟ almuwaẓẓaf: ṣabaahannoor ayya khidma
Mr Hassan: I want to open a joint account in my name and my wife's name.	السيد حسن : أريد فتح حساب مشترك، باسمى و اسم زوجتى . assayid ḥasan: ureedu fatḥa ḥisaab mushtarak be ismee wa isme zaujatee
Bank clerk: Have you filled this form and completed the formalities?	الموظف : هل ملأت هذه الاستمارة وأكملت الإجراءات ؟ almuwaẓẓaf: hal mala'ta haadhehil istaamaara wa akmalta alijraa'aat.
Mr Hassan: Yes, this is my signature and this is my wife's signature.	السيد حسن : نعم، هذا هو توقيعي وهذا هو توقيع زوجتي. assayid ḥasan: naʿam, ḥaadhaa huwa tauqeeʿee wa haadhaa huwa tauqeeʿ zaujatee
Bank clerk: Within a week we will send you a cheque book.	الموظف : خلال أسبوع سوف نرسل إليك دفتر شيكات. almuwaẓẓaf: khilaala usbooʿ saufa nursilu ilaika daftara shekaat

Mr Hassan: I want to encash this cheque also.	السيد حسن : أريد صرف هذا الشيك أيضا . assayid ḥasan: ureedu ṣarfa haadhashshek aiḍan.
Bank clerk: Please sign on the back of the cheque.	الموظف : وقّعْ على ظهر الشيك رجاءً . almuwaẓẓaf: waqqeᶜ ala zahreshsheek rajaa'an.
Mr Hassan: I also want to change Dollars.	السيد حسن : أريد أن أحوّل دولار أيضا . assayid ḥasan: ureedu an uḥawwila doolaar aidan.
Bank clerk: Please go to the foreign exchange counter.	الموظف : إذهب إلى شباك العملة الأجنبية . almuwaẓẓaf: idhhab ilaa shubbakil ᶜumla alajnabiyya
Mr Hassan: Please change these dollars to Indian rupees.	السيد حسن : أرجوك أن تحول هذا الدولار إلى روبية هندية . assayid ḥasan: arjooka an tuḥawwil haadha ddoolaar ilaa rubiya hindiyya.
Bank clerk: How many dollars do you have?	الموظف : كم دولار معك ؟ almuwaẓẓaf: kam doolaar maᶜaka?
Mr Hassan: I have one thousand dollars.	السيد حسن : معي ألف دولار . assayid ḥasan: maᶜee alf doolaar.
Bank clerk: Very well. Here are 35000 rupees.	الموظف : حسنًا، هذه (٣٥٠٠٠) روبية . almuwaẓẓaf: ḥasanan haadhihee khamsa wa thalaathoon alf rubiyya.

Mr Hassan: Thank you. السيد حسن : شكراً

assayid ḥasan: shukran

Bank clerk: Not at all. الموظف : عفوا

almuwaẓẓaf: ʿafwan

USEFUL VOCABULARIES

مفردات مفيدة

Bank	مصرف / بنك maṣraf / bank
Banking	أعمال مصرفية aʿmaal maṣrafiyya
Account	حساب ḥisaab
Current A/c	الحساب الجاري al hisaab aljaaree
Saving A/c	حساب توفير ḥisaab taufeer
Joint A/c	حساب مشترك ḥisaab mushtarak
Accountant	محاسب muḥaasib
Chartered accountant	محاسب قانوني muḥaasib qaanoonee
Calculator	حاسبة ḥaasiba
Bank statement	كشف الحسابات kashful ḥisaabaat
Balance	رصيد raṣeed
Fixed deposit	وديعة wadeeʿa
Receipt	إيصال / وصل waṣl / yeeṣaal
Cheque	شيك shek

Cheque book	دفتر شيكات daftar shekat
Passbook	دفتر الحساب daftarul ḥisaab
Bank draft	حوالة مصرفية ḥawaala maṣrafiyya
Traveller's cheque	شيك السياحة sheku ssiyaḥah
Customer	عميل ʿameel / زبون zaboon
To open an A/c	فتح حساب faṭḥu ḥisaab
To close	إغلاق ighlaaq
Delay	تأخير taakheer
Loan	قرض qarḍ
Invoice	فأتورة faatoora
Balance sheet	ميزانية meezaaniyya
Currency	عملة ʿumla
Hard currency	عملة صعبة ʿumla ṣaʿba
Foreign currency	عملة أجنبية ʿumla ajnabiyya
Bankrupt	مفلس muflis
Manager	مدير mudeer
Coupon	قسيمة qaseema
Renewal	تجديد tajdeed
Endorsement	تصديق taṣdeeq
Crossed cheque	شيك معنون shek muʿanwan
Exchange	تحويل taḥweel
Exchange rate	سعر التحويل seʿruttaḥweel
Buying rate	سعر الشراء seʿrushsheraa

Selling rate	سعر البيع seᶜrul baiᶜ
Bank note	ورقة نقدية waraqa naqadiyya
To encash	صرف ṣarf
Credit card	بطاقة الائتمان biṭaaaqatul i'tamaan
Small change	خردة khurda
Advance	سلفة sulfa
To withdraw	سحب saḥb
To pay	دفع dafᶜ
Letter of credit	رسالة الاعتماد risaalatul iᶜtamaad
Bill of exchange	كمبيالة kambiyaala
Bill of lading	سند الشحن sanadu shshaḥan

HOTEL

فُندق / funduq

Mr Hassan: Have you got a room for a week?	السيد حسن : هل عندك غرفة لمدة أسبوع؟ assayid ḥasan: hal ʿindaka ghurfa le muddate usbooʿ
Receptionist: Yes, you are most welcome.	موظف الاستقبال : نعم، أهلا وسهلا muwaẓẓafu istiqbaal: naʿam, ahlan wa sahlan
Mr Hassan: At first let me know what facilities are available with you.	السيد حسن : أود فى البداية أن أعرف التسهيلات المتوفرة لديكم assayid ḥasan: awaddu fil bidaaya an aʿrifa attasheelaat almutwaffira ladaikum
Receptionist: This is a big hotel.	موظف الاستقبال : هذا فندق كبير . muwaẓẓaful istiqbaal: haadhaa funduq kabeer
There are many rooms.	فيه غرف كثيرة . feehe ghuraf katheera
Each room has a bed and telephone.	وفى كل غرفة سرير وتلفون . wa fee kulle ghurfa sareer wa telfoon
It also has cold and hot water.	وبها أيضا ماء بارد وساخن . maa' baarid wa saakhin
There is a restaurant and bar in the hotel.	فى الفندق مطعم ومشرب . fil funduq maṭʿam wa mashrab

And there are other facilities as well.	وتوجد فيه تسهيلات أخرى أيضا. wa toojad feehe tasheelaat ukhra aiḍan
Mr Hassan: Give me a room facing the swimming pool.	السيد حسن : أعطني غرفة تطل على المسبح . assayid ḥasan: aᶜtenee ghurfa tutillu alal masbaḥ
Receptionist: I am sorry, all such rooms are engaged.	موظف الاستقبال : أنا آسف، مثل هذه الغرف كلها محجوزة . muwaẓẓaful isteqbaal: anna aasif, mithl haadhehil ghuraf kullihaa maḥjooza
Take any other room at the fourth floor.	خذ أي غرفة أخرى فى الطابق الرابع . khudh ayya ghurfa ukhra fiṭṭaabiq arraabe
Mr Hassan: What are the charges for one night?	السيد حسن : ما هى أجرة المنام لليلة واحدة ؟ assayid ḥasan: maa heya ujratul manaam le laila waḥida
Receptionist: Rs 1000 only.	موظف الاستقبال : ألف روبية فقط . muwaẓẓaful isteqbaal: alf roobiya faqaṭ
Mr Hassan: Is it inclusive of taxes also?	السيد حسن : هل هذا يشمل الضرائب أيضا ؟ assayid ḥasan: hal haadhaa yashmulu aḍḍaraayeb aidan
Receptionist: Yes.	موظف الاستقبال : نعم . muwaẓẓaful isteqbaal: naᶜam

Mr Hassan: What is check out time?	السيد حسن : ما هو وقت ترك الفندق ؟ assayid ḥasan: maa huwa waqtu tarkil funduq
Receptionist: 12:00 noon.	موظف الاستقبال : الساعة الثانية عشرة ظهرا . muwaẓẓaful isteqbaal: assaᶜa aththaaniyya ashara zuhran
Mr Hassan: Is there a lift in the hotel?	السيد حسن : هل يوجد مصعد فى الفندق؟ assayid ḥasan: hal yoojad miṣᶜad fil funduq
Receptionist: Of course.	موظف الاستقبال : طبعًا muwaẓẓaful isteqbal: ṭabᶜan
Mr Hassan: Then book for me one good room for one week.	السيد حسن : إذاً إحجز لي غرفة جيدة لمدة أسبوع . assayid ḥasan: iḍan iḥjaz lee ghurfa jayyida le muddate usbooᶜ
Receptionist: Any other service?	موظف الاستقبال : أي خدمة أخرى ؟ muwaẓẓaful isteqbaal: ayya khidma ukhra
Mr Hassan: Thank you.	السيد حسن : شكرا assayid ḥasan: shukran

USEFUL VOCABULARIES

مفردات مفيدة

Hotel	فندق funduq
5 Star Hotel	فندق ٥ نجوم funduq khamsa nujoom
Lounge	صالة الاستراحة ṣaatltul istaraaḥa
Cafeteria	مقهى maqhaa
Bar	مشرب mashrab
Restaurant	مطعم maṭᶜam
Theater	مسرح masraḥ
Self service	خدمة ذاتية khidma ẓaatiyya
Reservation	حجز ḥajz
Floor	طابق taabiq
Lift	مصعد miṣᶜad
Attached bathroom	غرفة بحمام خاص ghurfa beḥammam khaaṣ
Key	مفتاح miftaaḥ
Handing over of the key	تسليم المفتاح tasleemul miftaaḥ
Out of order	معطّل muᶜaṭṭal
Swimming Pool	مسبح masbaḥ
Laundry	مغسلة maghsala
Laundry service	خدمة الغسل khidmatul ghasl
Ironing	كيّ kayy
To change the sheets	تبديل الشراشف tabdeelu sh sharaashif
Checking in	دخول الفندق dukhuoolul funduq
Checking out	مغادرة الفندق mughaadaratul funduq

LOST PROPERTIES

المفقودات / almafqoodaat

Mr Hassan: Excuse me, sir!	السيد حسن: إسمح لي يا سيدي! assayid ḥasan: ismaḥ lee yaa sayyedee
Officer: Yes?	الموظف : نعم ؟ almuwaẓẓaf: naᶜam
Mr Hassan: Yesterday I have lost a black bag in the conference hall.	السيد حسن : لقد فقدت أمس حقيبة سوداء فى قاعة المؤتمر. assayid ḥasan: laqad faqaddtu ams haqeebaa saudaa'a fee qaᶜtil motamar
Officer: Have you forgotten it yesterday evening?	الموظف : هل نسيتها مساء أمس ؟ almuwaẓẓaf: hal naseetahaa masaa'a ams?
Mr Hassan: Yes, Sir.	السيد حسن : نعم، سيدي assayid ḥasan: naᶜam, sayyedee
Officer: Can you tell me what is inside it ?	الموظف : قل لي ما بداخلها ؟ almuwaẓẓaf: qul lee maa bedaakhilehaa?
Mr Hassan: Well, there is one file, one diary and two pens.	السيد حسن : حسناً، بداخلها ملف ومذكرة وقلمان . assayid ḥasan: ḥasanan, bedaakhilehaa milaff wa mudhakkira wa qalamaan.
Officer: Are you Mr Hassan?	الموظف : هل أنت السيد حسن ؟ almuwaẓẓaf: hal anta assayid ḥasan?

Mr Hassan: Yes, Sir.	السيد حسن : نعم، يا سيدي . assayid ḥasan: naʿam yaa sayyedee.
Officer: Here it is, but next time do not leave it like that.	الموظف : خذها، ولكن لا تترك مثل هذا فى المرة القادمة. almuwaẓẓaf: khudh haa, wa laakin laa tatruk mithla haadhaa fil marra alqaadimaa.
Mr Hassan: Thank you very much Sir, Goodbye.	السيد حسن : شكرا جزيلا يا سيدي، مع السلامة . assayid ḥasan: shukran jazeelan yaa sayyedee maʿassalaama.

DECLARATION OF A CAR THEFT
(at a police station)

تصريح بحادث سرقة السيارة

(فى مركز الشرطة)

taṣreeḥ beḥaadithe saraqatissayyara
(fee markazishshurta)

Mr Hassan: Good morning, Sir. My car has been stolen.	السيد حسن : صباح الخير يا سيدي . لقد سُرقت سيارتي. assayid ḥasan: ṣabaahal khair yaa sayyedee. Laqad sureqat sayyaratee.
Constable: From which place?	الشرطي : من أي مكان ؟ ashshurṭee: min ayee makaan?
Mr Hassan: Sadoon Street.	السيد حسن : شارع السعدون . assayid ḥasan: shaareʿ assʿdoon.
Constable: What time?	الشرطي: فى أي وقت ؟ ashshurṭee: fee ayee waqt?
Mr Hassan: At about 10'o clock in the night.	السيد حسن : بحوالى الساعة العاشرة ليلا . assayid ḥasan: beḥawaalai assaʿa alaaʿshira lailan.
Constable: What make is the car?	الشرطي: نوع السيارة ؟ ashshurṭee: nauʿu ssayyaara
Mr Hassan: Maruti.	السيد حسن : ماروتى assayid ḥasan: maarootee.
Constable: What colour?	الشرطي: لون السيارة ؟ ashshurṭee: launu ssayyara.
Mr Hassan: White.	السيد حسن : أبيض . assayid ḥasan:abyaḍ

Constable: Registration no.?	الشرطي: رقم التسجيل ؟ ashshurṭee: raqm uttasjeel
Mr Hassan: M4010.	السيد حسن : م ـ ٤٠١٠ assayid ḥasan: M - 4010
Constable: Do you have a driving licence?	الشرطي: هل عندك رخصة القيادة ؟ ashshurṭee: hal ʿindaka rukhṣatulqiyaada.
Mr Hassan: Yes, Sir.	السيد حسن : نعم يا سيدي . assayid ḥasan: naʿam, yaa sayyedee.
Constable: Okay, then leave your telephone no. and see us after two days.	الشرطي: حسناً، اعطني رقم تلفونك وراجعنا بعد يومين . ashshurṭee: ḥasanan, aʿtenee raqma telfoonika wa raajeʿnaa baʿda yaumain.

USEFUL VOCABULARIES

مفردات مفيدة

Description	وصف	waṣf
Black	أسود	aswad
Blue	أزرق	azraq
Green	أخضر	akhḍar
Grey	رمادى	ramaadee
Red	أحمر	aḥmar
Orange	برتقالى	burtaqaalee
Pink	وردى	waradee
White	أبيض	abyaḍ
Yellow	أصفر	aṣfar

RESTAURANT

مطعم / maṭᶜam

Mr Hassan: Give us the menu please.	السيد حسن : أحضر لنا قائمة الطعام من فضلك .
	assayid ḥasan: aḥḍir lanaa qaayamataṭṭaᶜaam min faḍlik.
Waiter: Here it is.	الجرسون: تفضل .
	aljarsoon: tafaḍḍal.
Mr Hassan: What is today's special dish?	السيد حسن : ما هو طبق اليوم؟
	assayid ḥasan: maa huwa ṭabaqulyaum
Waiter: Today's special dish is grilled meat.	الجرسون : طبق اليوم لحم مَشوِيّ .
	aljarsoon : ṭabaqul yaum laḥam mashwee
Mr Hassan: Have you got fish?	السيد حسن : هل عندكم سمك؟
	assayid ḥasan: hal ᶜindakum samak
Waiter: Yes, we have delicious fish.	الجرسون : نعم عندنا سمك لذيذ.
aljarsoon: naᶜam ᶜindanaa	samak laḍheedh
Mr Hassan: I will take a plate of fish, and you Arif?	السيد حسن : أنا آخذ طبق سمك وأنت يا عارف؟
	assayid ḥasan: anaa aakhudhu ṭabaqa samak wa anta yaa ᶜaarif?
Mr Arif: I will take baked potatoes and rice.	السيد عارف : أنا آخذ بطاطس بالفرن وأرزّ .
	assayid ᶜaarif: anaa aakhudu baṭaatis bilfurn wa aruẓẓ

Mr Hassan: First, bring us both tomato soup.	السيد حسن : أولا أحضر لنا شوربه طَماطِمْ لكل واحد .	assayid ḥasan: awwalan aḥḍir lanaa shouraba ṭamaaṭim lekulle waḥid
Mr Arif: Give us a plate of salad also.	السيد عارف : أعطنا طبق السَلَطَة أيضا .	assayid ʿaarif: aʿtenaa ṭabaqassalaṭaa aiḍan
Mr Hassan: What do you have for dessert?	السيد : ماذا عندكم فى الطبق الحلو ؟	assayid ḥasan: maadhaa ʿindakum fittabaq alḥulu
Waiter: We have fruits, and variety of pastries.	الجرسون : عندنا فواكه وفطائر مختلفة .	aljarsoon: ʿindanaa fawaakeh wa faṭaayar mukhtalifa
Mr Hassan: Do you have pastry filled with cream?	السيد حسن : هل عندكم كعك مملوء بالكريما ؟	assayid ḥasan: hal ʿindakum kaʿk mamloo'a bil kireemaa
Waiter: No, sir.	الجرسون : لا، يا سيدي .	aljarsoon: laa yaa sayyedee
Mr Arif: We will take fruits.	السيد عارف : نأخذ فواكه .	assayid ʿaarif: naakhudhu faakeha
Waiter: At the end, would you like to drink coffee?	الجرسون : وفى الأخير هل تشربون قهوة ؟	aljarsoon: wa fil akheer hal tashraboona qahwa

Mr Hassan : Yes, a cup of coffee for each, please.	السيد حسن : نعم، فنجان قهوة لكل واحد من فضلك . assayid ḥasan: naᶜam, finjaan qahwa lekulle waahid min faḍlik

USEFUL VOCABULARIES

مفردات مفيدة

Table	مائدة maayeda
Waiter	الجرسون aljarsoon
Plates	صحون/أطباق ṣuḥoon / aṭbaaq
Knife	سكين sikkeen
Fork	شوكة shauka
Spoon	مِلعقة milᶜaqa
Food	طعام ṭaᶜaam
Meal	أكلة akla
Juice	عصير ᶜaseer
Apple	تفاح tuffaaḥ
Orange	برتقال burtaqaal
Mango	منغا manghaa
Meat	لحم laḥam
Fish	سمك samak
Chicken	دجاج dajaaj
Rice	أرزّ aruzz
Vegetables	خضراوات khaḍrawaat
Salad	سلطة salaṭa

Fruits	فواكه fawaakeh
Fruit Salad	سلطة فواكه salaṭatu fwaakeh
Dessert	حلوى ḥalwa
Delicious	لذيذ ladheedh
Menu	قائمة الأطعمة qaayamatul aṭᶜema
Grilled meat	لحم مشوى laḥam mashwee
Baked potato	بطاطا بالفرن baṭaataa bilfurn
Bread	خبز khubz
Sweets	حلويات ḥalwiyyaat
Mixed Sweets	حلويات مشكلة ḥalwiyyaat mushakkala
Pastry	فطيرة faṭeera
Cake	كعكة kaᶜka
Waiter	جرسون jarsoon
Cup of tea	فنجان شاى finjaan shaay
Milk tea	شاى بالحليب shaay bil ḥaleeb
Lemon tea	شاى بالليمون shaay billaimoon
Roast chicken	دجاج بالفرن dajaaj bilfurn
Coffee	قهوة qahwa
Fruit-Juice	عصير فاكهة ᶜaseer faakeha
Cold water	ماء بارد maa'u baarid
Hot water	ماء ساخن maa'u saakhin
Breakfast	فطور fuṭoor

Lunch	غداء ghadaa
Dinner	عشاء ʿashaa
Bill	فاتورة faatoora
Tip	إكرامية ikraamiyya
Butter	زبدة zubda
Egg	بيضة baiḍa
Milk	حليب ḥaleeb
Sugar	سكر sukkar
Yoghurt	لبن laban
Salt	ملح milḥ

TELEPHONE

هاتف / تلفون haatif / telfoon

Directory	دليل daleel
Telephone directory	دليل الهاتف daleelul haatif
Telephone booth	كشك الهاتف العام kushkul haatif al^caam
Telephone exchange	بدالة الهاتف badaalatul haatif
PCO / ISD	مركز الاتصال المحلي والخارجي markazul itteṣaal almahallee walkhaarejee
Extension No.	تحويلة رقم taḥweela raqm
Intercom	نظام الاتصال الداخلي nizaamul itteṣaal addaakhelee
Code No.	رقم البدالة raqmul badaala
Mobile telephone	الهاتف النقال alhaatif annaqqaal
Dialling	إدارة قرص التلفون idaaratu qurṣittelfoon
Dialling tone	طنين التلفون ṭaneenuttelfoon
Dialling code	رقم البدالة raqmul baddaala
Busy	مشغول mashghool
Receiver	سماعة sammaa^ca
Number	رقم raqm
Call	مكالمة mukaalama
Local call	مكالمة محلية mukaalama maḥalleeya

Outside call	مكالمة خارجية mukaalama khaarjiyya
The line is busy.	الخط مشغول alkhaṭ mashghool
Sorry, wrong number.	آسف، الرقم غلط aasif, arraqm ghalaṭ
Who is speaking?	من يتكلم ؟ man yatakallam
This is Ali speaking.	أنا علي ۰ anaa ʿali
The telephone is out of order.	التلفون عاطل . attelfoon ʿaaṭil

THE HOUSE

البيت albait

House	بيت bait
Residence	سكن sakan
Apartment	شَقّة shaqqa
Building	مبنى mabnaa
Multi-storey	عمارة ʿimaara
Gate	باب رئيسي baab ra'eesee
Door	باب baab
Front door	باب أمامي baab amaamee
Back door	باب خلفي baab khalfee
Doormat	مِمسحة الأرجل mimsaḥatul arjul
Window	شباك shubbaak
Wall	جدار Jidaar
Balcony	شُرْفة shurfa
Roof	سقف saqaf
Room	غرفة ghurfa
Bed room	غرفة النوم ghurfatunnaum
Drawing-room	غرفة الاستقبال ghurfatul isteqbaal
Bathroom	حمّام ḥammam
Kitchen	مطبخ maṭbakh
Bed	سرير sareer
Curtain	ستار sitaar
Quilt	لحاف liḥaaf

Pillow	مخدة	mikhadda
Blanket	بطانية	baṭṭaaniya
Sheet	شرشف	sharshaf
Carpet	سجادة	sajjaada
Stairs	سُلَّمْ	sullam
Lock	قفل	qufl
Key	مفتاح	miftaaḥ
Bucket	دلو	dalw
Furniture	أثاث	athaath
Chair	كرسي	kursee
Table	مائدة	maayeda
Sofa	أريكة	areeka
Cupboard	دولاب	doolaab
Shelf	رفّ	raff
Mirror	مرآة	mir'a
Fan	مروحة	mirwaḥa
Bulb	مصباح كهربائي	miṣbaaḥ kahrabaayee
Switch	مفتاح	miftaaḥ
Television	تلفزيون	telfizyoon
Video	فيديو	feedeo
Refrigerator	ثلاجة	thallaaja
Deep freezer	مجمدة	mujammeda
Air conditioner	مكيف الهواء	mukayyefulhawa

Air Cooler	مبرّد الهواء mubarridulhawa
Geyser	سخان الماء sakhkhaanul maaye
Toilet	مرافق maraafiq
Bell	جرس jaras
Mosquito net	ناموسية naamoosiyya
Iron	مكواة mikwa
Vacuum cleaner	مكنسة كهربائية miknasa kahrabaayea

USEFUL PHRASES

العبارات المفيدة / alᶜibaaraat almufeeda

Come (msc)	تعال taᶜaal
Come (fem)	تعالي taᶜaalee
Come here	تعال هنا taᶜaal hunaa
Come back	إرجع irjeᶜ
Come tomorrow	تعال بكرا taᶜaal bukra
Go	رُحْ ruḥ
Go away	رح من هنا ruḥ min hunaa
Get out	اطلع برا iṭlaᶜ barra
Speak	تكلم takallam
Bring me	هات لي haate lee
Take	خذ Khudh
Call him	ناديه naadeehe
Get up	قم qum
Say	قل qul
Tell me	قل لي qul lee
Look here	أنظر هنا unzur hunaa
Be careful	إحذر iḥdhar
Listen to me	إسمعني ismaᶜnee
Stop it	وقفه waqqifhu
Do not go	لا ترح laa taruḥ
Do not come	لا تجئ laa taje'
Do not be afraid	لا تخف laa takhaf
Do not forget	لا تنس laa tansa
Do not tell him	لا تقل له laa taqul lahu
Do not mention it	لا تذكره laa tadhkurhu

Car parking area — موقف السيارات mauqefussayyaraat

No parking — ممنوع الوقوف mamnooʿul wuqoof

No entry — ممنوع الدخول mamnooʿuddukhool

No smoking — ممنوع التدخين mamnooʿuttadkheen

Beware of dogs — إحذر الكلاب iḥdhar alkilaab

Emergencies — طوارئ ṭawaaree

Emergency exit — باب الطوارئ babuṭṭawaaree

Special — خاص khaaṣ

Private — خاص khaaṣ

Pin — دبُوس dabboos

Scissors — مقص miqaṣṣ

Stapler — مِدبسة / كابسة kaabisa / midbasa

Hour — ساعة saaʿa

Minute — دقيقة daqeeqa

Second — ثانية thaaneya

Morning — صبح ṣubḥ

Noon — ظهر ẓuhr

After noon — بعد الظهر baʿda ẓẓuhr

Evening — مساء massaa

Night — ليل lail

Midnight — منتصف الليل muntaṣafullail

Today — اليوم alyaum

Tomorrow — بكرة bukra

Yesterday — أمس ams

RELATIVES

أقارب / aqaarib

Father	والِدْ / أبْ waalid / ab
Grandfather	جَدْ jad
Mother	أمْ um
Grandmother	جَدَّة jadda
Brother	أخ akh
Sister	اُخت ukht
Husband	زوج zauj
Wife	زوجة zauja
Uncle	عم ʿam
Aunt	عمة ʿamma
Son	إبن ibn
Daughter	بنت bint
Grandson	حفيد ḥafeed
Father-in-law	حَمُوْ ḥamu
Mother-in-law	حَمَاْة ḥamaat
Son-in-law	صهر ṣihr
Daughter-in-law	زوجة الابن zaujatul ibn
Twins	توأمان tau'amaan
Inheritor	وارث waarith
Nephew	ابن الأخ ibnul akh

DAYS OF THE WEEK

أيام الأسبوع / ayyaamulusboo'

Sunday	يوم الأحد yaumul aḥad
Monday	يوم الإثنين yaumul ithnain
Tuesday	يوم الثلاثاء yaumuththulathaa
Wednesday	يوم الأربعاء yaumul arbi'aa
Thursday	يوم الخميس yaumul khamees
Friday	يوم الجمعة yaumul jum'a
Saturday	يوم السبت yaumussabt

TIMING

التوقيت / attauqeet

What time is it now?	كم الساعة الآن ؟ kamissaaʿa alaan?
It is nine o'clock.	الآن الساعة التاسعة . alaan assaaʿa attaasiʿa.
It is five minutes past nine o'clock.	الآن الساعة التاسعة وخمس دقائق . alaan assaʿ attaasiʿa wa khamsa daqaayeq.
It is quarter past nine.	الآن الساعة التاسعة والربع . alaan assaʿ attaasiʿa wa rrubʿa
It is half past nine o'clock.	الآن الساعة التاسعة والنصف . alaan assaʿ attaasiʿa wa nnusf.
It is quarter to ten o'clock.	الآن الساعة العاشرة إلا الربع . alaan assaʿ alaashira illarrubʿa.

MONTHS OF THE YEAR

شهور السنة / shuhoorussana

January	يناير/ كانونُ الثاني yanaayar / kanoonu ththaanee
February	فبراير / شُباط febraayar / shubaaṭ
March	مارس / آذار maars/ aadhaar
April	إبريل / نيسان abreel/ neessan
May	مايو / أيار maayoo/ ayyaar
June	يونيو / حزيران yooneo/ ḥazeeraan
July	يوليو / تموز yooleo/ tammooz
August	اُغسطس / آب ughusṭus/ aab
September	سبتمبر / أيلول sebtembar / ailool
October	أكتوبر/ تشرين الأول uktoobar/ tishreenul awwal
November	نوفمبر / تشرين الثاني naufambar / tishreenuth thaanee
December	ديسمبر / كانونُ الأول deesembar/ kanoonul awwal

THE HUMAN BODY
جسم الإنسان / jismul insaan

Arm	ذِرَاع dhiraaʿ
Back	ظَهْر zahr
Belly	بَطْن baṭn
Cheek	خَدّ khadd
Chest	صَدْر ṣadr
Ear	أُذْن udhn
Eye	عَيْن ʿain
Face	وَجْه wajh
Finger	إِصْبَعْ iṣbaʿ
Foot	رِجْل rijl
Hair	شَعْر shaʿr
Hand	يَدْ yad
Head	رأسْ raas
Heart	قَلْبْ qalb
Mouth	فَمْ fam
Nose	أنْف anf
Shoulder	كَتْف katf
Skin	جِلْدْ jild
Tongue	لِسَانْ lesaan
Teeth	أسْنَان asnaan

FRUITS

فواكه fawaakeh

Apricot	مِشْمِشْ mishmish
Apple	تُفّاح tuffaaḥ
Banana	مَوْز mauz
Cherry	كرز karaz
Coconut	جَوْز الهند jauzul hind
Date	تَمَرْ tamar
Fig	تين teen
Groundnut / Peanut	فول سوداني fool soodaanee
Grapes	عنب ʿinab
Lemon	ليمون laimoon
Mango	منغا manghaa
Peach	خوخ khookh
Strawberry	فراولة farawala
Pear	إجّاص ijjaaṣ
Plum	برقوق burqooq
Pine apple	أناناس anaanaas
Papaya	ثمرالبيو thamarul beyo
Lichee	اللتشية allitshiya
Walnut	جوز Jauz
Grapefruit	كريب فروت kareeb froot

VEGETABLES
الخضروات / alkhaḍrawaat

Bean	فَاصُولْيَا faaṣooliya
Beetroot	شمندر shamandar
Carrot	جَزَرْ jazar
Cabbage	كرنب kurunb
Cauliflower	قرنبيط qarnabeet
Cucumber	خيار khiyaar
Eggplant	باذنجان baadhinjaan
Pea	بازِلاً baazilla
Potato	بطَاطَا baṭaaṭaa
Marrow	كوسا kosaa
Lettuce	خسْ khas
Okra	بَامِيَا baamiya
Onion	بَصَلْ baṣal
Mushroom	فُطْر fuṭr
Tomato	طَمَاطِم ṭamaaṭim
Garlic	ثوْم thoom

COUNTRIES

البلدان / albuldaan

Afghanistan	افغانستان afghaanistaan
Albania	البانيا albaaniya
Algeria	الجزائر aljaẓaayar
Angola	أنغولا anghoolaa
Argentina	الأرجنتين alarjanteen
Australia	أستراليا ustraaliyaa
Austria	النمسا annimsaa
Bahamas	البهاما albahaamaa
Bahrain	البحرين albaḥrain
Barbados	بربادوس barbaadoos
Belgium	بلجيكا beljeekaa
Bermuda	برمودة barmoodaa
Bhutan	بوتان bootaan
Bolivia	بوليفيا booleefiya
Brazil	البرازيل albrazeel
Bulgaria	بلغاريا bulghaariya
Burma	بورما booramaa
Burundi	بوروندى booroondee
Cambodia	كمبوديا kambodiya
Cameroon	الكميرون alkameroon
Canada	كندا kanadaa
Chad	تشاد chaad
Chile	شيلى sheelee

China	الصين aṣṣeen
Colombia	كولمبيا kolombiya
Congo	الكونغو al-kongo
Costa Rica	كوستاريكا koostaareekaa
Cuba	كوبا kooba
Cyprus	قبرص qubrus
Czechoslovakia	تشكوسلوفاكيا cheekoslofaakiya
Denmark	الدنمارك addenmaark
Dominica	الدومينيكان addomeenikaan
Ecuador	إكوادور ikwaadoor
Egypt	مصر miṣr
El Salvador	السلفادور assalfaadoor
Ethiopia	أثيوبيا athyoobiya
Fiji	فيجى feejee
Finland	فنلندا finlandaa
France	فرنسا faransa
Gabon	الغابون alghaaboon
Gambia	غامبيا ghaambiya
German Democratic Republic	جمهورية المانيا الديمقراطية jumhooriyyatu almaaniya addimuqraatiya
Federal Republic of Germany	المانيا الاتحادية almaaniya alittehaadiya
Ghana	غانا ghaanaa

Great Britain	بريطانيا العظمى breeṭaaniya aluzma
Greece	اليونان alyoonaan
Guatemala	غواتيمالا ghuwaateemaalaa
Guinea	غينيا gheeniyaa
Guyana	غيانا ghayanaa
Haiti	هاييتى ḥaayeettee
Holland	هولندة holanda
Honduras	هندوراس hinduraas
Hong Kong	هونغ كونغ hong kong
Hungary	المجر almajar
Iceland	أيسلندة aislanda
India	الهند alhind
Indonesia	إندونسيا indonesia
Iran	إيران iraan
Iraq	العراق alᶜiraaq
The Republic of Ireland	جمهورية إيرلندة jumhuriyatu earlanda
Italy	إيطاليا yeeṭaaliya
Jamaica	جمايكا jamaayekaa
Japan	اليابان alyaabaan
Jordan	الأردن alurdun
Kenya	كينيا keneeya
Korea	كوريا kooriyaa
Kuwait	الكويت alkuwait

Laos	لاؤس	laoos
Lebanan	لبنان	lubnaan
Lesotho	ليسوثو	leesoothoo
Liberia	ليبريا	leebeeriya
Libya	ليبيا	leebiya
Luxemburg	لوكسمبرغ	loksumbargh
Madagascar	مدغشقر	madaghashqar
Malawi	مالاوى	maalaawee
Malaysia	ماليزيا	maleezia
Mali	مالى	maalee
Malta	مالطة	maalṭaa
Mauritania	موريتانيا	moreetaaniyaa
Mauritius	موريشيوس	moreeshyoos
Mexico	المكسيك	almekseek
Mongolia	منغوليا	mangholiya
Morocco	المغرب	almaghrib
Mozambique	موزمبيق	mozambeeq
Nepal	نيبال	neebaal
New Zealand	نيوزيلندة	neuzeelanda
Nicaragua	نكاراغوا	nekaraghua
Niger	النيجر	annaijar
Nigeria	نيجيريا	naijeeriya
Norway	النرويج	annarweej
Oman	عمان	ʿomaan
Pakistan	باكستان	baakistaan

Palestine	فلسطين falasteen
Panama	بنما banamaa
Paraguay	باراغواى baaraaghuway
Peru	بيرو beeru
Philippines	الفيليبين alfeeleebeen
Poland	بولندة bolanda
Portugal	البرتغال alburtaghaal
Qatar	قطر qaṭar
Rhodesia	روديسيا roodeesia
Romania	رومانيا roomaaniya
Russia	روسيا roosiya
Saudi Arabia	السعودية assaʿudiya
Senegal	السنغال assinighaal
(The) Seychelles	سيشيل sesheel
Sierra Leone	سيراليون seeraa loon
Singapore	سنغافورة singhafoora
Somalia	الصومال aṣṣoomaal
South Africa	جنوب إفريقيا junoob ifreeqiya
Spain	أسبانيا asbaaniyaa
Sri Lanka	سريلانكا sireelaankaa
Sudan	السودان assudaan
Swaziland	سوازيلاندا suwaazeelanda
Sweden	السويد assuwaid
Switzerland	سويسر suwaisraa

Syria	سوريا sooriya
Taiwan	تايوان taiwaan
Tanzania	تنزانيا tanẓaaniya
Thailand	تايلاند tailand
Tibet	التبت attibat
Tobago	توباغ toobagh
Togo	توغو tooghoo
Trinidad	ترينيداد treeneedaad
Tunisia	تونس toonis
Turkey	تركيا turkiya
Uganda	أوغندا ughandaa
USSR	اتحاد الجمهوريات الاشتراكية السوفيتية ittihaadul jumhooriyaat alishtaraakiyya assaufeetiyya
Uruguay	أورغواى urooghuway
Venezuela	فنزويلا fenzuweelaa
Vietnam	فيتنام feeṭnaam
(The) West Indies	الهند الغربية alhind algharbiyaa
Yemen	اليمن al yaman
Yugoslavia	يوغسلافيا yoghuslaafiya
Zaire	زائير zaayeer
Zambia	زامبيا zaambiya
Zimbabwe	زمبابوى zembabwey